A YEAR AT THE HELM OF THE
UNITED NATIONS GENERAL ASSEMBLY

A Year at the Helm of the United Nations General Assembly

A Vision for Our Century

Nassir Abdulaziz Al-Nasser

Edited by Shara Kay

WITH A FOREWORD BY BAN KI-MOON

NEW YORK UNIVERSITY PRESS
New York and London

NEW YORK UNIVERSITY PRESS
New York and London
www.nyupress.org

References to Internet websites (URLs) were accurate at the time of writing.
Neither the author nor New York University Press is responsible for URLs
that may have expired or changed since the manuscript was prepared.

Library of Congress Cataloging-in-Publication Data
Al-Nasser, Nassir Abdulaziz.
A year at the helm of the United Nations General Assembly : a vision for
our century / Nassir Abdulaziz Al-Nasser ; with a foreword by Ban Ki-moon.
pages   cm
Includes bibliographical references and index.
ISBN 978-1-4798-6200-9 (cl : alk. paper)
1. United Nations. General Assembly (66th session : 2011–2012) 2. International
relations—Moral and ethical aspects. 3. Conflict management—International
cooperation. 4. Pacific settlement of international disputes. 5. Natural disasters—
Prevention—International cooperation. 6. Sustainable development—
International cooperation. 7. Human security—International cooperation.
8. World politics—2015–2015. I. Title.
JZ5006.2.A5 2014
341.23'22—dc23   2013049736

New York University Press books are printed on acid-free paper,
and their binding materials are chosen for strength and durability.
We strive to use environmentally responsible suppliers and materials
to the greatest extent possible in publishing our books.

Manufactured in the United States of America

10 9 8 7 6 5 4 3 2 1

Also available as an ebook

To my son, Aziz, and all the children of the world

CONTENTS

FOREWORD

Ambassador Nassir Abdulaziz Al-Nasser of Qatar presided over a dynamic year in the United Nations General Assembly. This volume offers a comprehensive account of his engagement, reflecting discussions on a range of global challenges.

The September 2011 high-level season was one of the busiest ever, with special meetings on nuclear safety and security, global health threats, counterterrorism and sustainable development, and talks on Libya and the Horn of Africa.

Following those discussions, President Al-Nasser and I traveled to Libya, Somalia, and Kenya to show solidarity with the people. In Libya, we met senior officials and leaders of civil society groups. We paid our respects at the site of mass graves. In Somalia and Kenya, we held talks with transitional leaders, African Union commanders and troops, relief workers, and refugees.

Well before Ambassador Al-Nasser's election as president of the General Assembly, he appreciated the special role of the General Assembly. He once declared, "An enduring characteristic of this Organization is that—irrespective of the political and practical changes—the General Assembly remains its most inclusive body." I share this esteem and have always endeavored to work closely with the Assembly president to address global challenges.

I am pleased that Mr. Al-Nasser remains in the United Nations family as high representative of the Alliance of Civilizations. As he brings his expertise and leadership to this new role, I am confident readers

will find in these pages worthwhile information on his recent experience presiding over the "world's parliament"—the General Assembly of
the United Nations.

BAN KI-MOON
Secretary-General of the United Nations
March 31, 2013

After two decades of experience in the diplomatic corps at the United Nations, I had the honor and privilege of serving as the president of the General Assembly (PGA) for the 66th session, which began September 13, 2011, and ended September 17, 2012.

My primary job as PGA was as a mediator and a facilitator. I worked closely with all member states to help find common understanding and to promote consensus in intergovernmental negotiations. The role of the president also involves many formal, ceremonial, and diplomatic functions. One such function is to lead discussions in General Assembly meetings. Another is to enhance the visibility of the Assembly worldwide.[1]

The 66th session of the General Assembly took place at a critical juncture in the history of nations. People across the globe were questioning their systems of governance—no longer afraid to ask for what they deserve—and actively seeking change. The environment was reacting to human mistreatment, striking back with seemingly endless natural disasters and ensuing humanitarian crises. The world economy was facing the most serious financial crisis since the Great Depression, threatening to destabilize livelihoods and undermining global efforts for growth and prosperity.

Future generations would hold the UN accountable for how we responded to these critical issues. This decisive moment in history was our opportunity to prove that we, the international community, had the courage, wisdom, and tenacity to seek creative and visionary solutions;

that we could work together to produce results; that we had learned the lessons of the past; and that, when faced with those few who choose force and brutality, we would choose peace, human rights, and democracy.[2]

* * *

How did I come to lead the General Assembly, the world's most representative body, at this crucial moment in history? It was a long journey filled with challenges, hard work, and compromise.

I am the oldest child in my family. Even as a small boy, I had big dreams. At the age of fourteen, I tried to start a company. I asked my father to finance the enterprise, but he told me if I wanted to be a businessman, I should study hard and make money for myself. I was disappointed, but I kept dreaming.

My next plan was to attend military college, specifically the Royal Military Academy Sandhurst (RMAS) in England. It was very prestigious and controlled by the British government. At that time, RMAS gave out two scholarships a year to Qatar. In 1972, when I graduated high school, the first scholarship went to the son of the foreign minister. The other one went to me: a dream come true.

A few days later, my father and I visited the foreign minister. The minister asked me to join the ministry of foreign affairs. Qatar had just become independent. We did not have many qualified diplomats. I was surprised because I had not yet finished university, but the minister suggested that I could get my degree while working as a junior diplomat.

I struggled to make up my mind. I was only seventeen years old. I asked my father for advice, but he told me I had to be responsible for my own decision. After sleeping on it, I decided to accept the minister's offer. In the morning, I went to the ministry of foreign affairs and told him I was ready. I would begin work the very next day. Would I receive a diplomatic passport? I asked. "Of course," the minister answered, laughing. "That is your only concern? I am trying to help you with your future!"

That lucky decision led me where I am today. My journey as a diplomat began in Beirut, then Pakistan; then I became consul general in Dubai; and from Dubai, I was sent to the UN as deputy permanent representative. The transition was not easy, but I welcomed the challenges of multilateral diplomacy.

In 1993, I returned to bilateral diplomacy as the ambassador of Qatar to Jordan. It was a difficult moment after the invasion of Kuwait, and the relationship between my country and Jordan was not great. But it seemed God was on my side. With instruction from my government, I had the chance to improve the relationship, and Qatar and Jordan became very close. I also became the dean of Jordan's diplomatic corps. After five years, as a reward for what I had achieved in Jordan, I was sent back to the UN as permanent representative of my country.

This was 1998. I was in the right place at the right time: Qatar foreign policy was becoming very active around the world. My country contributed a lot to the work of the UN on different issues and then became nonpermanent member of the Security Council for the 2006–2007 session, during which we played a significant role. I had the opportunity to serve as president of the Security Council for one month in December 2006. Because it was the last month of the year, my office dealt with a number of very important issues.

Before and after my time on the Security Council, I was elected by member states to preside over a number of important UN organizations including the Group of 77 and China (G-77), the High-Level Committee on South-South Cooperation, and the Fourth Committee of the UN General Assembly (also known as the Special Political and Decolonization Committee). I also served as vice president of the General Assembly in 2002.

In 2010, after thirteen years of service as permanent representative of Qatar to the UN, my country nominated me as a candidate for the presidency of the General Assembly, which rotates between the five regional groups (Asia and the Pacific, Africa, eastern Europe, Latin America and the Caribbean, and western Europe and others).[3] For the 66th session, the turn fell to the Asia and Pacific group. It was a tough campaign, as there was a second candidate nominated, so we conducted a vote within the group. Fortunately, drawing on my experience and my reputation among member states, I managed to win this preliminary vote, and I went on to win the general election by acclamation. In June 2011, I left the mission of Qatar, and in September, I began my new position as president of the General Assembly. It was a year I will never forget.

* * *

I identified four main areas of focus to help frame the work of the 66th session. Each of these pillars is elaborated in a subsequent chapter of this book. The text is largely drawn from the speeches I delivered during my term, with the addition of new anecdotes and reflections on my experiences. For those who are interested in reading the speeches as I originally delivered them, the notes will point you to the relevant archived page on the United Nations website. For readers less familiar with the UN system, the notes also contain background information on certain UN institutions and issues. I have also indicated where to find sources and documents that I reference, such as resolutions of the General Assembly.

I would like to thank my friend and special adviser, Professor Mustapha Tlili of New York University, for the inspiration to create this record of my work. I have often relied on Professor Tlili's wise input during my term and now in my new function of United Nations high representative for the Alliance of Civilizations, for which he serves as my senior adviser.

I am also grateful to Shara Kay for editing this book, weaving a year's worth of my communications and memories into a well-organized and coherent narrative. For valuable research help, my thanks go as well to Edoardo Bellando, information officer, United Nations.

On March 1, 2013, with the support of my country and the cofounders Spain and Turkey, I assumed a new mandate as the UN high representative for the Alliance of Civilizations. I firmly believe that global efforts toward peace and reconciliation can only succeed when our collective approach is built on trust, dialogue, and collaboration. Realizing this need, the United Nations established the Alliance of Civilizations as a soft-power tool to promote dialogue for peace and development. During my presidency of the General Assembly, and to set an example for the vision I believe in, I attended several events at which we discussed and promoted cross-cultural dialogue as a crucial component in our efforts to build peace, tolerance, harmony, and mutual understanding around the world. As high representative for the Alliance of Civilizations, I welcome the opportunity to continue working to further the noble goals of the Alliance to preserve international peace and security and to strengthen relations between nations and cultures. It is a responsibility I take very seriously.

As president of the 66th session, I determined to leave behind a stronger General Assembly that the people of the world can look up to and depend on. We achieved quite a lot, but I am mindful of the fact that there is only so much that can be accomplished in a one-year term.[4] I hope this book will shed light on the important work of the General Assembly and that future General Assembly presidents will continue to enhance the visibility of the office.

INTRODUCTION

Ambassador Al-Nasser brought to the presidency of the 66th UN General Assembly the rich store of diplomatic experience that he had accrued as a representative of his country in different state capitals, notably in the Middle East and Asia. As he took on the complex and demanding responsibilities of the UNGA presidency, and the multifaceted tasks of the United Nations, he will have reflected on the usefulness of his experience in the Qatari representation in New York from 1986 to 1993 and his return to the United Nations as ambassador and permanent representative in 1998.

Ambassador Al-Nasser's intimate knowledge and long experience of the workings of international diplomacy served him well during what proved to be an exceptionally busy and challenging year for the Assembly and indeed for the international system as a whole. The UN, like any international body, is only as effective as its members will allow; decision-making can be tortuous and slow. Ambassador Al-Nasser brought to the presidency of the 66th UNGA genuine enthusiasm and persistence in the face of bureaucratic obstacles, as well as expertise, especially in the areas of peace and security, South-South relations, and sustainable development.

It was a particularly apt circumstance that, in a year in which many of the world's priority political challenges arose from the wave of change sweeping the Arab World, the General Assembly had at its head a natural interpreter of these events, with an intimate understanding of Arab history and culture. The need for immediate responses to upheaval in

Syria, but also North Africa, is an important theme running through the year and through this volume. Outcomes often fell below Ambassador Al-Nasser's hopes and expectations, and he puts them in the context of the multiplicity of other issues and challenges with which the UN must grapple each session.

Ambassador Al-Nasser was ambitious for his presidency and wanted the 66th UNGA not only to focus on the emergencies and ongoing crises in this turbulent world but also to identify, and keep energies trained on, the priorities that he termed his "Four Pillars." These were

- the peaceful settlement of disputes;
- reform and revitalization of the UN system;
- disaster prevention and response; and
- sustainable development and prosperity.

He approached these major concerns and goals at two levels: by contributing to ongoing efforts to improve UN systems to deliver improved responses in the future and by working to maximize the impact of current interventions. For example, in the area of United Nations reform, while arguing for the modernization of membership of the Security Council, he also set out to attempt to make the interplay between institutions within the UN more effective and responsive: a bold task indeed.

This volume will, I believe, be a resource for future scholars. It will undoubtedly attract the interest also of others who focus on international affairs, in particular the role of the United Nations and of its most representative body, the General Assembly. The UNGA is, after all, the only forum in the world where all the world's nations can take part, in principle equally, in the running of our planet's affairs. It is at the same time essential but unwieldy and difficult to manage—legitimate but not always decisive or authoritative—even with an experienced president at the helm. The book also usefully reminds us of the huge number of issues that face the international community and the forbidding and intractable nature of some of them.

Ambassador Al-Nasser brings to this range of issues his skill and expertise and an engaging conviction in the vital necessity of international cooperation in our increasingly interdependent world. He advocates a positive, optimistic approach to the promotion of the fundamental human values that are, albeit expressed in local idioms, common to all faiths and cultures. This book can only scratch the surface of a busy and eventful year. The reader can only imagine the continuous, intricate, and relentless toil that promoting this agenda must have entailed—even to organize the meetings and orient them, one day at a time, toward the establishment of a consensus.

In this book, Ambassador Al-Nasser has provided us with a host of insights into the work of the United Nations and his role in it. Given the man's energy and commitment, it is no surprise that, following his presidency of the UNGA, he was appointed further high international responsibilities, which he carries with distinction today, as UN high representative for the Alliance of Civilizations. This post is well suited to his diplomatic talents and will enable him to continue to play an influential role in championing the noble values he sets out with such clarity and conviction in this memoir.

DR. FARHAN NIZAMI, CBE
Prince of Wales Fellow, Magdalen College, Oxford
Director, Oxford Centre for Islamic Studies

1

A Vision for Universal Values

In 1945, the leaders of the world came together in San Francisco and signed the United Nations Charter. They did so in the belief that every nation can advance its own interests by building common ground with the interests of others and that the whole of our power is greater than the sum of its parts. The United Nations is an organization that illustrates that the yearning for peace is a universal search and that universal peace requires universal solutions.

The desire of humankind for universal values can be traced back to the oldest times of humanity, whether through religion or philosophy. These values were described by Plato as objective: the Good, the True, and the Beautiful. Ever since, philosophers—including classical Muslim philosophers such as Averroes, Avicenna, and Ibn Khaldoun, to name a few—have considered these values the basis for bridging our differences and bringing us together in one human community.

The most striking and brilliant expression of these ambitions may have found its achievement in the writing of Immanuel Kant. It is said that when President Woodrow Wilson was reflecting on the future of humanity after the disaster of World War One, one of his most relied on readings was Kant's essay "Perpetual Peace."[1] These readings infused the spirit of the treaty that gave birth to the League of Nations.

The UN Charter, born after the tragedy of World War Two, took up this challenge again, striving to bring us ever closer to the desire for those universal values. Signed on June 26, 1945, at the conclusion of the United Nations Conference on International Organization in San Francisco, it outlines the goals of the organization—to "save succeeding generations from the scourge of war," "to reaffirm faith in the . . . dignity and worth of the human person [and] in the equal rights of men and women," and "to promote social progress and better standards of life in larger freedom."[2] It is a hard road that we still pursue today, even after the adoption of the Universal Declaration of Human Rights in 1948.[3]

It is no secret that, in some parts of the world, the United Nations has suffered an image problem in recent years. Indeed, there has been a perception among some people that the UN is irrelevant in today's global world. Ironic, is it not? The UN—the most global, interconnected organization in the world—irrelevant in today's global, interconnected world?

This view has grown largely from within conservative camps in some Western countries and their media. Yet we must admit that the world has indeed changed since the UN's establishment in 1945. At the time the UN was born, 750 million people—almost one-third of the world's population—lived in colonized territories. More than half of the world was not represented at the UN. Self-determination was but a far-off dream.

Since that day, more than eighty former colonies have gained their independence. Hundreds of millions of people have realized their passionate yearning for freedom. This has changed the makeup of the United Nations as well. We have grown from 51 member states in 1945 to 193 in 2012.

Today, we face a world again in transition—a transition like none seen since the end of decolonization. Take the issue of race, for instance. It has moved from being framed as an apartheid question to how to build multiethnic, multicultural, pluralistic societies. Take another example—the climate issue. Those who spoke about it only twenty years ago were tentative in their assessments and predictions. Today, science tells us that climate change is one of the major challenges the international community must face.

Take the issue of democracy. Who would have thought, even five years ago, that the quest for democracy would become the central focus of the Arab people. Who could have imagined the strong calls for freedom, dignity, and justice of all those who today are celebrating what is widely called the "Arab Spring" and what I prefer to call the "Arab Awakening." Indeed, just as the world experienced a major transition immediately after World War Two, we find ourselves today also going through a historic transition, with all the challenges and hopes it implies.

And so what is the UN's role today? What can the UN offer in response to the challenges of our times, and how effective are we in that response? I submit that the United Nations' role is more important than ever before. In today's Internet-driven world, where we live side by side with those who are oceans apart, we must act in a way that respects and embraces our shared values and collective efforts.

The UN is the expression of our common journey and—let us be frank—our mutual dependence. It is a place where all the major problems of the world find their destination. It is a place where all the hopes of humanity converge for a better tomorrow.

Take the world economy. At the heart of our economic challenges are the issues of demand versus resources. How do we provide economic justice so that the world can live and progress in greater harmony? The gap between rich and poor is growing. Economic growth is weak, and the global economic system is fragile. And everything is compounded by increasingly depleted natural resources. Addressing poverty is of course key to achieving economic and social justice.

The UN provides the space for our concerted efforts to grow and to achieve justice. The United Nations Millennium Development Goals (MDGs), stemming from the 2005 World Summit attended by more than 170 heads of state and government, offer a blueprint for development.[4] The MDGs offer a policy framework agreed to by all the world's countries and leading development institutions.[5]

Eight goals have been set: from halving extreme poverty to ensuring environmental sustainability to stopping the spread of HIV/AIDS.[6]

The target date for the MDGs is 2015. Since their launch in 2000, the MDGs have galvanized never-before-seen efforts to meet the needs of the world's poorest populations. There is no doubt that important progress has been made toward most MDG targets.[7]

Consider another critical issue: the responsibility to protect, or "R2P" in UN speak. Following the tragedies in Rwanda and the Balkans in the 1990s, the international community began to debate how to react when citizens' human rights are grossly violated. Did states have unconditional sovereignty over their affairs? Or had the international community the right to intervene in a country for humanitarian purposes?[8]

In the Millennium Report of 2000, UN Secretary-General Kofi Annan, recalling the failures of the Security Council to act in a decisive manner in Rwanda and the former Yugoslavia, put forward a challenge to member states: "If humanitarian intervention is, indeed, an unacceptable assault on sovereignty, how should we respond to a Rwanda, to a Srebrenica, to gross and systematic violation of human rights that offend every precept of our common humanity?"[9]

The expression "responsibility to protect" was first presented in the report of the International Commission on Intervention and State Sovereignty, set up by the Canadian government in 2001 in response to the secretary-general's question. The report proposed that when a state fails to protect its people—through lack of ability or lack of willingness—the responsibility shifts to the international community.[10]

In 2004, the High-Level Panel on Threats, Challenges and Change, set up by the secretary-general, endorsed the norm of a responsibility to protect, stating that there is a collective international responsibility, "exercisable by the Security Council authorizing military intervention as a last resort, in the event of genocide and other large-scale killing, ethnic cleansing and serious violations of humanitarian law which sovereign governments have proved powerless or unwilling to prevent."[11] The panel proposed basic criteria that would legitimize the authorization of the use of force by the Council, including the seriousness of the threat, the fact that it must be a last resort, and the proportionality of the response. The secretary-general "strongly agreed" with this approach in his 2005 report "In Larger Freedom"; he suggested that a list of proposed criteria—including seriousness of the threat, proportionality, and chance of success—be applied for the authorization of the use of force.[12]

At the United Nations World Summit in 2005, all member states accepted the responsibility of each state to protect its population from genocide, war crimes, ethnic cleansing, and crimes against humanity.[13] They also agreed that when any state fails to meet that responsibility, the international community is responsible for helping to protect people threatened with such crimes. Should peaceful means—including diplomatic, humanitarian, and others—be inadequate and national authorities "manifestly fail" to protect their populations, the international community should act collectively, on a case-by-case basis, through the Security Council and in accordance with the United Nations Charter.

The Security Council has applied that principle in practice, authorizing the deployment of peacekeeping troops to Darfur, the Sudan, in 2006. More recently, we have seen the critical role of R2P in Libya. We have seen the Security Council's timely and resolute response in the face of an imminent threat of mass atrocities. And we have seen the UN's central role as a moral authority—a moral authority against the gross and systematic violation of human rights.

While some people have raised questions about whether NATO overstepped its mandate in Libya, this does not change the normative reach of the R2P concept or the UN's responsibility to act. It was, and it remains, clear to all that there could not be silence in the face of such brutality.

I am offering these examples to illustrate what can be achieved when 193 nations agree to act and to show that, despite nations' cultural, social, economic, historical, and political particularities, some truths are self-evident and universal. They apply everywhere. They are universal values, as described in the UN Charter and the Universal Declaration of Human Rights.[14]

The General Assembly

Underpinning our efforts at the United Nations is a shared, interfaith belief in the inherent goodness of every individual and our commitment to peace, forgiveness, and compassion. Consider for a moment:

In Christianity, it is said, "Do to others what you would like others to do to you."

In Islam, we hear, "Wish for others what you wish for yourself."

In Judaism, we learn, "What is hateful to you, do not do to your neighbor."

In Buddhism, it is declared, "Treat not others in ways that you yourself would find hurtful."

And in Hinduism, we hear, "Do not do to others what would cause pain if done to you."

At the heart of the United Nations are these very values, common to us all. Our organization is the ideal forum whereby we can start to make peace within ourselves, within our families, and between our communities and our nations.[15] Because universality is not a given; 193 countries implies 193 governments, 193 national economies. And how many historical experiences! And how many national interests![16]

Much of the UN's work to build consensus takes place in the General Assembly. The UN Charter established the Assembly as the UN's chief deliberative and policymaking body. Unlike any other international institution, the General Assembly is arguably the most universal, legitimate, representative body in the world: 193 member states; one country, one vote. Big and small countries, rich and poor—all count equally inside the General Assembly Hall.

The Assembly is tasked to consider the full spectrum of international issues covered by the UN Charter—from international peace and security to human rights to development. Decisions of the Assembly provide a global voice to major concerns of our time. The General Assembly also provides a place—*the* place, some might say—for the world to connect.

Every September, as the citizens of New York are all too aware, 193 heads of state and government and other senior officials, as well as thousands of delegates, meet at UN Headquarters. Despite appearances, the Assembly in this high-level week is much more than a talk shop. Global agendas are set. Paths forward are mapped. Commitments are made.

And it is quite thrilling, yet humbling, to be in the General Assembly Hall with hundreds of representatives from around the world. You hear it all—from English to Hiri Motu to Swahili. Such a gathering reminds you of just what the world has to offer and what the UN has to offer the world.

Let me give you another example of what we can accomplish when the community of nations comes together. In September 2011, for the first time ever, world leaders recognized that noncommunicable diseases (NCDs)—heart disease, cancer, chronic lung diseases, and diabetes—have reached epidemic proportions. We agreed to act. The international community committed itself to developing national capacities for addressing NCDs and to strengthening national NCDs policies and plans.

There is power in these collective commitments. They offer support to governments in developing policies. They also create space for sharing ideas and best practices, such as using low-cost, cost-effective interventions to build an effective national response to tobacco use. By creating a global agenda, ideas grow and governments and communities are more empowered to follow a path that works.[17]

Four Pillars

For six months—between my election as PGA in February and taking office in September—I worked to shape the agenda of the 66th session according to my own priorities and the concerns expressed to me by member states. I narrowed these down to four pillars that would guide our work; each is the focus of a later chapter of this book. Together, these ideas represent my vision for achieving stable and prosperous democracies; continued growth and development; and the protection and promotion of human rights for the citizens of the world.

We organized at least one high-level policy meeting on each pillar. In preparation, I selected two permanent representatives of countries actively involved in that issue to serve as cofacilitators and sent a letter to all member states encouraging them to exchange ideas with these ambassadors. The cofacilitators would negotiate with regional groups about their views and attempt to produce a consensus document. As PGA, I worked hard to achieve a positive atmosphere, but of course, we were more successful in some areas than in others; it is not always possible to reach compromise between member states with widely different agendas and points of view.

The first pillar is the peaceful settlement of disputes. History has shown that peaceful settlements of disputes, including those brokered through mediation efforts, provide the most cost-effective and long-lasting solutions. And in today's world, the need to find peaceful resolution to disputes has become more relevant and urgent than ever. For this reason, I selected the theme "The Role of Mediation in the Settlement of Disputes" for the 66th session's General Debate. (Though no actual debate takes place, the so-called General Debate is the most important meeting of the session, during which the Assembly is addressed by heads of state and government from all over the world.)[18]

Qatar, though it is a small country, is very active in mediation. As permanent representative, I was involved in efforts to broker solutions to political and military conflicts in Sudan, Darfur, Yemen, Lebanon, and elsewhere in Asia and Africa. These experiences, coupled with my time on the Security Council, convinced me of the value of mediation, whereas the use of force to settle disputes will often backfire, creating even greater instability. Since the very founding of the UN, mediation has been one of its key tools for creating international peace and security, with a specific reference in the United Nations Charter.[19]

Accordingly, the United Nations Alliance of Civilizations at the global level is extremely important and can help to resolve differences between states with widely disparate cultures. It can be used to strengthen dialogue, rapprochement, and development, which will, in turn, help to strengthen coexistence and thus forge international peace and security.

Here, I should like to proudly mention the leading role that my country, Qatar, has played in supporting the Alliance and its strategic aims. I have taken upon myself to practice and promote the Alliance's mission as part of my work in the United Nations, including as the permanent representative of Qatar to the United Nations. It is therefore no wonder that the issue of the Alliance of Civilizations and its relationship to mediation in the settlement of disputes should be the first of my priorities while president of the General Assembly. Subsequently, as UN high representative for the Alliance, I have added mediation as a pillar of the Alliance's mission.

The Alliance of Civilizations is one of the most innovative endeavors of the international community, aiming to provide the world with a framework for mending our differences and building common ground for a human family that is more tolerant and peaceful at a time of historical change. That Alliance proved its effectiveness when tensions rose after 2001 and has proved to be a new path to peace for the United Nations to follow.

This method can be applied not only to conventional conflicts but also to multifaceted confrontations and tense relationships that include, for example, Iran and the West over the nuclear issue. Few people would disagree that the security and stability of the Gulf region are central to the security and stability of the whole world.[20]

In the past few years, the use of mediation and other tools of peaceful means has gained momentum within the United Nations and in many regions around the world. In the preceding (65th) session, the General Assembly had adopted its first ever resolution on mediation.[21] With this resolution, the General Assembly took an important step in affirming support for strengthening mediation as a vital tool for conflict prevention and resolution.[22]

My intention for the 66th session was not only to sustain the work that came before but also to increase its momentum. It is my view that the General Assembly should, through its revitalization, become more engaged and empowered on issues of mediation, so that it can fulfill its role as the world's preeminent peacemaker at this major juncture in international relations.[23]

During the General Debate, many delegations welcomed this theme and reflected on the increasing role of mediation and prevention. Examples were shared of mediation efforts from member states' own regions. It was acknowledged that mediation is a cost-effective tool and that regional and subregional organizations play a vital role in the peaceful solution of conflicts. Member states noted that the full and effective participation of women in mediation efforts is vital and that the involvement of civil society is becoming increasingly important. And there was widespread support for the secretary-general's efforts in conflict prevention and calls for UN capabilities in this respect to be enhanced.[24]

The second pillar is UN reform and revitalization. The UN is built on strong foundations, but its institutions were designed almost seventy years ago in the aftermath of World War Two. Today, our world is much more interdependent, complex, and fast-paced. Change is essential in the cycle of life, and there is no shame in recognizing that after six decades, the UN—particularly its Security Council—needs reform.[25]

Charged by the UN Charter with the maintenance of international peace and security, the Security Council deals with some of the most urgent and pressing global issues. Its responsibilities, among others, include investigating disputes which may lead to international friction, recommending action on threats to peace, and taking military action against an aggressor.

The membership of the Council is well known: five permanent members with the power to veto decisions and ten nonpermanent members, without the power to veto. The structure was established in 1945 with eleven Security Council members out of forty-five total member states and enlarged to fifteen members in 1965 by an amendment to the Charter.[26] But does this membership reflect the global realities of today? I do not think there is anyone in the UN Hall who would argue that it does.

Today we have new centers of power such as the BRICS—the expanding powerhouses of Brazil, Russia, India, China, and South Africa. The past decade or so has seen efforts to adjust the International Monetary Fund (IMF) voting structure to reflect the new power realities—and this is only natural and, I would say, just. Unlike the United Nations General Assembly, where each country has one vote, decision-making at the IMF was designed to reflect the relative positions of its member countries in the global economy. Each country is assigned a quota based on that position. This quota determines a member's maximum financial commitment to the IMF and its voting power and has a bearing on its access to IMF financing. Reforms are under way to reflect the larger role played by emerging markets and developing economies. Following the entry into effect of the 2008 Amendment on Voice and Participation on March 3, 2011, quota and voting shares will change as eligible members pay their quota increases.[27]

How long, then, can the world wait without the necessary reform of the Security Council? My answer is, not much longer. For history has shown that international organizations face their most critical moments when they fail to respond to dynamic changing environments. What will the situation be if we do not achieve progress on this front? Could the United Nations and the international community bear the consequences? My answer is, no.

The legitimacy of the United Nations' mission will be undermined in the absence of an efficient, inclusive, and representative Security Council. Timely reform is urgent if the United Nations is to respond to twenty-first-century realities. However, to attain real progress, reform must be fully driven and defined by the member states.[28] The General Debate witnessed broad agreement on the urgent need for early consensual reform of the Security Council. Such reform is inevitable if the Council is to reflect contemporary realities.[29]

I aimed to use my presidency to build on previous efforts to reform the Security Council and, harnessing the collective will of the membership, advance them further. I set out to foster stronger interaction and genuine balance between the General Assembly, the secretary-general, the Security Council, and the UN's Economic and Social Council (ECOSOC) in dealing with issues of peace and security, according to the respective mandates defined by the Charter.[30]

Let it be noted here that ECOSOC has a very clear role under the UN Charter: the harmonization of the economic and social interests of the international community. For those who have witnessed the limitations of other economic forums, I would reiterate: exclusion does not solve economic problems. It simply delays and worsens them. As president, I appealed to those who were leading efforts through various negotiating forums to heed the call of universal interests and to make greater use of instruments such as ECOSOC.[31]

In the wake of the world financial and economic crisis, improving global economic governance has increasingly been viewed as critical for assuring greater international financial stability. Global governance should go beyond crisis management and should be capable of anticipating, as well as addressing, emerging medium- and long-term issues. By the same token, relevant global institutions—above all the UN—should be able to respond to the new challenges of globalization and the realities of the twenty-first century.[32]

Has progress been made toward UN reform? Recent initiatives for reducing overlap, embracing innovation, and building greater synergies are steps in the right direction. However, it cannot be overemphasized that the United Nations cannot function effectively unless it is provided with necessary resources, both human and financial.[33] Of particular importance is supporting the Assembly to respond, at an early stage, to emerging situations of common concern to the international community. In order to remain legitimate, it is also important that there is strong political will to realize previous resolutions and decisions of the Assembly.[34]

The third pillar of my vision is improving disaster prevention and response. The world has experienced an unprecedented surge of natural and man-made disasters in recent years. The 2011 earthquake and tsunami in Japan were a dire warning that even the most technologically advanced nations are susceptible to unforeseen effects of severe weather events. The Earth's temperature is rising, tectonic plates are shifting, and many lands are drying up. Populations across the world are experiencing increased vulnerability, food insecurity, and health and education crises. Disasters may be either man-made or natural and do not differentiate between developing or developed countries. Experience has shown beyond all doubt that natural disasters can strike mercilessly on the most highly developed states, on fertile and barren areas, on rich and poor, great and small.[35]

To address these critical issues, we must enhance cooperation among various actors. We must invest in preparedness and take greater efforts to reduce risk and vulnerability to natural hazards. Rather than wait to act in the aftermath of disasters, I believe the UN should focus more on building the capacities of vulnerable regions to make them more capable and self-reliant. As president of the Assembly, I also urged the UN to provide full moral and financial support to help restore peace and security in Somalia, where the people are facing starvation and humanitarian disaster on an unimaginable scale.

During the General Debate, many member states expressed grave concern for the humanitarian crisis in the Horn of Africa. This crisis was identified as a major threat to stability and prosperity in region.[36] The Security Council subsequently adopted a resolution that increased troop levels in Somalia by more than five thousand as well as increasing its logistical support package.[37]

While certain achievements have been made, there are new and ongoing crises requiring our attention. We must recognize that humanitarian issues are development issues and that our success in protecting against natural hazards will have a direct impact on our ability to fulfill the Millennium Development Goals. I remain committed to strengthening the

UN's response efforts and to becoming more coordinated and holistic in our approach.

The fourth pillar is sustainable development and global prosperity. This is also a key pillar of the work of the secretary-general, His Excellency Mr. Ban Ki-moon. We both believe strongly in the need to balance the economic, social, and environmental aspects of sustainable development with human beings at the center of our efforts. On the issue of climate change, a key priority is safeguarding the human rights of people whose lives are most adversely affected by the Earth's rising temperature. This challenge can only be effectively addressed through a partnership between developing and developed countries premised on the principle of common but differentiated responsibilities.

Sustainable development was particularly high on the agenda of the 66th session as we prepared to meet in Brazil for Rio+20 (Earth Summit). My team and I, with the help of member states, worked very hard to make that conference a success. The global economic crisis had created difficult conditions for compromise. The donor countries, such as the U.S., Europe, and Japan, would have to weigh the needs of less developed countries facing poverty, disease, corruption, and instability against their own domestic financial considerations. I was genuinely worried that we would not be able to produce an outcome document in Brazil, but through patient negotiation, we arrived at a compromise that would maintain the previous level of commitments.

Several other important gatherings on sustainable development took place during the 66th session, as well, including the High-Level Meeting on Desertification and the tenth session of the Conference of the Parties (COP 10) to the UN Convention to Combat Desertification (UNCCD), which was held in the Republic of Korea. At both of these meetings, I urged world leaders to take strong and urgent action for the protection of the global climate, for present and future generations. The year 2011 also marked the tenth anniversary of the New Partnership for Africa's Development, a vital framework for helping to address poverty and

underdevelopment throughout Africa. With the target date for achieving the MDGs on the horizon, and as we face global economic turmoil,
improving global governance and finding innovative financing modalities will continue to be high on our agenda. As the secretary-general
has said on several occasions, the major groups should come together
to solve the global financial crisis—no one can fix this issue alone—and
the UN should be the central forum for its discussion.[38]

In accordance with the powers granted to me in the final communi-
qué of the Earth Summit, I also worked toward establishing a mechanism within the General Assembly that will define the new development
goals for 2015 and beyond, to be known as the Sustainable Development
Goals.[39] I formed a team of members states to undertake that task, in
accordance with the usual system of geographical distribution. I was
very happy to be undertaking this historic duty.[40]

While I intended these four pillars to provide a framework to focus
the efforts of the UN's 66th session, there were of course many more
issues to address, including the Comprehensive Convention on International Terrorism and strengthening the UN's peace-building architecture. It was also an important year for the issue of disarmament,
particularly nuclear disarmament, which remains a prominent and
ever-more-pressing priority for the UN. Key meetings on disarmament during my term included the UN Conference on the Arms Trade
Treaty and a review of the UN Programme of Action on small arms and
light weapons.[41]

It must be acknowledged that the issue of Palestine was crucial to
the session as well. I endeavored to work with all member states for the
attainment of a just and comprehensive negotiated peace settlement in
the Middle East, based on a two-state solution.[42] Though we obviously
did not achieve that goal during my term, we witnessed the renewed
hope and reaffirmed determination of the Palestinian people. It was
indeed a historic moment when President Mahmoud Abbas announced
that he had submitted an application to the secretary-general for the

admission of Palestine to the United Nations.[43] I received an identical request in my capacity as president of the General Assembly and immediately circulated it to all member states. We are all aware that the passage of that request was blocked in the Security Council, for political rather than technical or legal considerations. However, in November 2012, the General Assembly upgraded the Palestinian Authority to "nonmember observer state" status.[44] Of course, beyond the issue of representation of Palestine at the United Nations, the Middle East must eventually become free of occupation and of nuclear weapons and be secure from wars and the evils of conflict.[45]

No member state can face these global challenges alone. We will need strong collaboration and consensus building to move forward. Key to success are both South-South cooperation—the exchange of resources, technology, and knowledge between developing countries, also known as countries of the global South—and triangular cooperation, which normally involves a traditional donor from the ranks of the Development Assistance Committee of the Organization for Economic Cooperation and Development (OECD), an emerging donor in the South, and a beneficiary country in the South.[46] In this regard, it will be vital to strengthen the current UN institutional mechanisms for South-South cooperation, including the Special Unit for South-South Cooperation.[47]

It is also key to ensure interaction between the General Assembly and civil society, nongovernmental organizations, and the private sector. There can be no dialogue without civil society. Civil society is an important partner for UN member states. To engage with the processes of the General Assembly, there are a number of important mechanisms available to civil society. One forum that has proven helpful in the past is civil society hearings. Here, civil society actors not only identify and report on situations of common concern; they also make recommendations that are given due weight when decisions of the membership are made. Other opportunities for engagement include the work of the Assembly's main committees and events mandated by the Assembly, such as commemorative meetings.[48]

The Arab Awakening

I was fortunate to serve as PGA at an essential moment in international affairs, a historic and unforgettable moment in the history of the Arab world. We welcomed the new leaders who came to the UN Hall to ask the international community to assist in the fulfillment of their populations' aspirations for the rule of law, transparency, prosperity, justice, and human rights.[49] The UN Charter and the Universal Declaration of Human Rights reaffirm these fundamental rights: the worth of the human person; the equal rights of men and women, of nations large and small; our joint obligation to ensure justice and respect for international law.

Francis Fukuyama put it remarkably, in famous if often misunderstood terms, speaking of "the end of history."[50] What Fukuyama argued powerfully was that liberal democracy and its values are the endpoint of humanity's sociocultural evolution, that in liberal democracy we have reached the ultimate form of organizing social life, of articulating the social contract. Of course, I concede that there are particularities in given societies, but it is possible always to strive constructively toward the utmost level of universality.[51]

Cultural relativism has no place here. Those who say that the Universal Declaration of Human Rights has its limitations are cultural relativists. And cultural relativism is a dead end. For who can, in all moral and intellectual honesty, argue anything other than equality? Other than dignity for all?

This is also what, in reality, unites the world of Islam and the West, despite claims to the contrary. But let us first define what we are speaking about when we speak of "Islam" and "the West." Let us make clear that we are not speaking of homogeneous entities but of diverse worlds on both sides.

But for the sake of exposition, let us assume that these are clearly defined camps. And with this assumption, let us then recognize that the competition between the two civilizations is as old as the advent of

Islam: what Professor Mustapha Tlili terms "the new kid on the block," the first two being Judaism and Christianity.[52]

Historically, that competition has been peaceful at times, violent at others, but overall extremely productive and to the benefit of human-kind's advancement. Philosophy, science, technology, state adminis-tration, army organization, and many other fields of human progress would not be what they are today without this dynamic relationship.

So let us not forget this important truth. And let those who agitate the specter of confrontation, of a clash of civilizations, remember that within these three faiths and within these three civilizations, what is common far exceeds what is different.

If we find ourselves today experiencing moments of tension, par-ticularly since the ugly terrorist attacks of the past decade—in New York, London, Madrid, and other places where senseless violence has struck—this should not cloud our judgment or make us believe that confrontation is an inevitable fate.

There is no inevitability of a clash of civilizations between the West and Islam. It is not a clash of values; it is a clash of perceptions. Muslim as well as Western philosophers uphold the same values of compassion and justice. There was a time when the two traditions nurtured each other, as beautifully described in the great book *The Ornament of the World* by Maria Menocal.[53]

Today, the Arab world is undergoing a period of profound change unlike any since the decolonization era. People across the Arab world are taking action and speaking with voices previously unheard.[54] Before young Tunisian Mohamed Bouazizi immolated himself for freedom and dignity, who could have imagined such historic change?[55]

The protesters in Tunisia were the educated sons and daughters of the large middle class, built over decades under the historic leadership of those who liberated Tunisia from colonialism. The protesters' demands reflected the very essence of this history. Their aspirations have become a cry of protest for revolutionaries the world over, who are taking their destinies into their own hands, in the Arab world and beyond, from

Libya to Egypt, Yemen and Syria; from Wall Street to Red Square; and who knows where else tomorrow.[56]

But, I must confess, I am concerned. I am concerned about how these legitimate aspirations, these hopes, these dreams, will be transformed into real reform and long-lasting change. I am concerned about how it will be ensured that the pendulum that has now swung away from tyranny, corruption, and oppression—toward freedom, transparency, and dignity—will stay where it rightly belongs. How can we ensure that the pendulum will not swing back or be hijacked by movements with self-interested or unconstructive ideologies?

New democracies in the region are now in a critical transitional phase. At the fore are vital questions on how to execute political and economic reforms. Indeed, this is a moment of significant challenge but, more importantly, of great opportunity: a moment when functioning, efficient, representative governments can be built; a moment when greater accountability, transparency, and the rule of law can be institutionalized; and a moment when the rights of women, youth, and minorities can be entrenched.

The key question facing me as PGA was, how can the United Nations best provide support and assistance to member states making the transition to democratic governance? The UN has a key role to play in mobilizing political will and international support for these countries facing the challenges of transition. It also has a long and vast experience in providing capacity-building support, such as electoral assistance and support for effective aid management. The UN expeditiously sent assessment missions to evaluate the needs and offer UN expertise in Tunisia, Egypt, and of course Libya.

But we also must recognize that democratic transformation needs to be coupled with economic transformation. Economic exclusion—including a lack of decent work and opportunity—is arguably one of the driving forces behind the Arab Awakenings.

Let me share with you a bit of history, although it is condensed. Many Arab nations, following their independence, adopted a development model based on the intervention of the state. Over time, state-led development policies, and the public provision of basic social services, came to form an integral part of the Arab social contract. These policies, in some cases, contributed to the emergence of a middle class. Eventually, however, for macroeconomic reasons, this model was gradually replaced by large-scale privatization of public assets.

The downside of this new model was threefold: first, politically well-connected individuals got richer; second, public officials became less accountable; and third, widespread economic inefficiency and inequality grew. The dysfunction of the model was such that asset concentration in the region is today a glaringly visible phenomenon. Meanwhile, a large and increasing number of the urban poor cluster in areas without sanitation, recreational facilities, reliable electricity, or other basic services. Unemployment rates among youth in Arab states are twice the global average.

Unfortunately, economic growth in the region has not, to date, led to a significant reduction of poverty and inequality. There is a critical need for building more inclusive economies throughout the Arab world: economies that will raise living standards and create sustained job growth; economies that are geared to the interests of peoples and are protected from corrupt practices; in a few words, economies that will uphold the ideals of justice and dignity for all.

To do so, the wealth generated by extractive industries in countries rich in resources must be employed for the benefit of all. To do so, fiscal revenues should be used to finance development policies. To do so, corrupt practices should be, once and for all, eradicated. To do so, the rule of law must become the rule of the land.

Carrying out economic reform in times of political upheaval is, no doubt, challenging. But leaders of the region must make the necessary effort despite these challenges. No one doubts that a sound economy can much improve the prospects of a democratic transition.

But let us not hide the truth from ourselves. Tough developmental and fiscal choices in the Arab region can only be made by responsive and accountable governments—governments that represent the needs and aspirations of the many, not the few.

The international community must help this process in every way that it can. The international community can assist directly, through political support and technical cooperation. The international community can also assist indirectly, through providing a macroeconomic context favorable to the success of development efforts in the region. I would emphasize, however, that national ownership is key.

Let me now move from economic reform to a second topic: education. We know that education is a basic human right, enshrined in the Universal Declaration of Human Rights. We know that education is fundamental to development, growth, and poverty eradication. We know that education is central to the achievement of the Millennium Development Goals. There is no doubt that the Arab world has made progress in improving the education of its people. The entire Middle East North Africa (MENA) region has increased its expenditure in this sector, as a percentage both of public spending and of GDP.

Yet illiteracy and massive unemployment persist. There is a shortage of qualified teachers. UNESCO estimates that the Arab world will need an additional 450,000 teachers by 2015. Overall, the World Economic Forum's Global Competitiveness Report 2010–2011 found that most countries in the MENA region score low on the quality of education and training.

Providing access to quality education, including for girls, should therefore be among the top priorities of governments in the region. Here, too, the international community can play a supportive role by strengthening the sustainability of funding for national education systems. Such sustained funding will provide more and better-equipped classrooms, as well as more qualified teachers.

My third theme relates to the political sphere. I have already touched on the need for accountable governance. Accountable governance is one of the most significant expressions of good governance. And good governance is central to ensuring that the voices of the people, expressed in legitimate, democratic ways, are heard, considered, and respected.

But, of course, elections are not enough. What is needed is a culture of democracy in the Arab world—a culture in which the peaceful selection of a country's leaders is the norm, not the exception, a culture in which mutual respect among citizens of different views is intrinsic to the civic mindset.

This transformation toward a culture of democracy takes time. It is a long, challenging process, in which citizens need to learn how to emphasize plurality and diversity: plurality of opinion and ideas, diversity of faith and ethnicity. They need to learn how to build political spaces that can peacefully accommodate the diverse components of civil society and how to be inclusive, not resort to demonization or exclusion.

In the end, these societies will need to learn how to eradicate violence from the political sphere and enshrine the peaceful workings of democracy as a civic culture. This transformation, I repeat, will take time, but it is fundamental to democracy and to answering people's calls for representative, functioning, efficient governments.

I would reaffirm here that, in undertaking the UN's work, there is no one-size-fits-all model for reform. The international community must respond to the needs as presented by the concerned populations, to ensure that true ownership and legitimacy are the way forward.

Let me now turn to the topic of security. Today, security concerns in the Middle East are largely dictated by the following factors: first, a stalled peace process; second, a blocked and ever-growing threat of nuclear proliferation; and third, conflicting national approaches to security.

It is safe to say that we do not know yet exactly how the new regional dynamics in the Arab world will reflect on states' approaches to these three issues. What we can say with a fair amount of certainty is that these new regional dynamics will have some impact on the emergence of a new—or at least a different—political order in the Middle East.

In my view, to ensure the future and the stability of the region, we have to work harder to find a solution to the Israeli-Palestinian conflict. The Palestinians cannot be left untouched by these winds of change. It is in the interest of the Israelis and the Palestinians that the parties come back to the negotiating table. The international community must also work harder on a solution in Syria that will meet the legitimate aspirations of the Syrian people.

I would now turn to the topic of culture. I am an Arab, proud of the achievements and civilization that the Arab world built over centuries. However, I have to be frank with you. Today, the Arab world is largely absent from the forces moving the world in science, technology, the arts, music, literature, and other fields of creativity. With very few exceptions, the current landscape is desolate. This is the sad truth, testified to by the United Nations Human Development Reports, the annual publications commissioned by the United Nations Development Programme (UNDP). (Innovative in their methodology and often provocative in their conclusions, the reports were launched in 1990 with the goal of putting people at the center of development. Contributors include leading development scholars and practitioners, working under the coordination of the UNDP Human Development Report Office.)[57]

Arabs would once again excel if their highly qualified sons and daughters—who today contribute, as exiles, to the development of science and technology in Silicon Valley, to the brilliance of literature and fashion in Paris and London—would find themselves comfortable in political and social settings in their home countries, in which they would reclaim the status of the region as an ornament of the world, the way it was in times past. This is possible today, with the dawn of democracy.

The region would once again excel if its affirmation of universal values, of the Universal Declaration of Human Rights, is total and unqualified by any cultural relativism or other restriction.

The region would once again excel if freedom of thought, freedom of expression, freedom of religion, freedom of conscience, and full gender equality are the unrestricted rule of the land, upheld by all institutions of government, and nurtured by civil society as a culture.

The premises of democratization, of openness, of transparency, of the rule of law, of universal values are there to give the region a chance at joining the movement of history. The Arab Awakening is an opportunity to be part of the global village and the modern world and to contribute to their progress, through providing the world not only with energy resources but also with universally acclaimed products of the mind.

Let me now dream with you and try to imagine what the Arab world will look like ten or fifteen years from now, when my young son will be an active citizen. If all goes well:

> If Palestinians and Israelis live in peace and harmony, in two states recognized by the world community and integrated into the region
>
> If a nuclear-weapon-free Middle East is finally achieved
>
> If solid democratic institutions are built to sustain and manage the normal political life of a peaceful, participatory democracy
>
> If investment in modern education and culture take the lead in the setting of national priorities
>
> If the Arab world pools its enormous natural resources and its efforts and puts them in the service of collective regional development
>
> If openness, tolerance, transparency, the rule of law, justice, freedom of thought, freedom of information, and freedom of expression become embedded in the civic culture

If all these challenging yet possible outcomes are realized, then I can see an Arab world reconciled with itself and with modernity. I can see a Middle East and North Africa becoming the land in which civilization again blossoms and offers the world that which only this great region offered throughout history: a mix of a good life and spiritual elevation, where the holy land as the birthplace of three great Abrahamic faiths becomes also the source of a new modernity, aligning the material and the spiritual.[58]

The Arab world has before it a golden opportunity to reclaim its region as a cradle of tolerance, innovation, and civilization. Let us join together to make sure these noble aspirations become an everyday reality—ordinary, not exceptional—for the people of the Arab world.[59] This is the path that Harun al-Rashid and al-Ma'mun through Bait el Hikma charted for us. This is what we can achieve in our own time.[60]

A Hyperconnected World

I believe our optimism must be balanced with an awareness of the very real challenges and threats facing humanity today.

At any given period in history, we can point to enclaves of poverty, be they small or large; to territories in conflict, be they local or regional; to inequality of various degrees. This is to say, injustice and inequity are not new. They have been part of humankind's journey since the dawn of time.

I suspect you would, however, agree with me that there are very few periods in the world's history during which there was as much conflict and tension; as many competing aspirations, with their resulting instability; as much conspicuous consumption and inequality; in a few words, as much dysfunction as there is in the global world of today.

What also makes today truly unique is that we are no longer concerned just by our family, just by our village, or just by our nation-state. In this deeply interconnected planet, what concerns one concerns all. The challenges belonging to one group belong to us all.

The UN is by its Charter a forum whose purpose is "to unite our strength to maintain international peace and security" and "to practice tolerance and live together in peace with one another as good neighbours."[61] These are apt words for a world where we are now all neighbors—where we all face shared, extraordinary challenges.

It used to be that we would hear about a catastrophe in Japan years after it happened. There would be little impact on others' perceptions and lives. Imagine, for instance, the plague that erased most of Europe in the fourteenth century. Then, the impact on China was not registered. Events would be local, perhaps regional at most.

But today, immediacy is the postulate of our lives to the extent that sometimes we live events before they happen—through rumors or "news" going viral on the Internet and through social media.

In the age of the Internet, history cannot define events in the same way it did before. Without social media, the drama set off by young Tunisian Mohamed Bouazizi would have been limited to his hometown. It would not have affected the region and the world, setting off a most profound chain of events.

And Occupy Wall Street? A small group of activists in New York City set off a worldwide protest movement. Now, common parlance speaks of "the 99 percent." It is likely that this "supraconnection" through social media will only continue as technologies advance and improve.

So we are moving. The challenge is how to understand the implications of qualitative change and their full potential for solving crises and increasing the opportunities to work together. How can heads of state make thoughtful and accurate decisions in a world where these decisions might not make sense minutes after they are made?

Accidents happen. If, when states are involved, accidents are misinterpreted, it can lead to catastrophe. If the world was saved from nuclear destruction during the Cold War, it was because the Soviet Union and the United States kept secret channels of communication to gauge each other's true intentions. This we know today; it is part of the historical record. In these times of tensions between the U.S. and Iran, I would call for the setting up of a similar channel of communication to avoid a simple yet catastrophic misunderstanding.

What role can the United Nations play in building more harmonious lives for the global community, using the communication tools at our disposal?

Here, too, let me call your attention to this truth that so many tend to forget: the UN has been at the origins of the global communications revolution. It has led the way, through the organization's various bodies, ranging from the Committee on the Peaceful Uses of Outer Space established in 1959 to the Committee on Information, which deals with questions relating to public information,[62] to the International Telecommunication Union (ITU), the UN specialized agency for information and communication technologies. Headquartered in Geneva, ITU allocates the global radio spectrum and satellite orbits, develops the technical standards that ensure that networks and technologies seamlessly interconnect, and strives to improve access to information technology to underserved communities worldwide. ITU has a membership of 193 countries and more than 700 private-sector entities and academic institutions.[63] The seventy-four-member United Nations Committee on the Peaceful Uses of Outer Space reviews the scope of international cooperation in peaceful uses of outer space, devises programs to be undertaken under UN auspices, encourages research and the dissemination of information, and addresses legal problems arising from the exploration of outer space.[64]

Through all these bodies, the main concern of the United Nations has been—and remains here, too—justice.

How do we implement justice in the digital arena and prevent division in the world between the digital haves and have-nots?

How do we give access to communication satellites to those in the developing world who cannot afford what rich and powerful countries can afford, either in launching their own satellites or buying use time?

How do we benefit from the advances in Internet technology in a way that no population is left behind?

You will concur with me that our future—the future of humanity, the future world in which my young son will live—will be, whether we like it or not, dominated by digital communications.

I call on all responsible members of the international community to think seriously about gathering all actors—state, private sector, academic, and corporate—to hold a world forum to consider all the possibilities of this future and to prepare a blueprint for a more coherent, effective, and just system that will benefit all and will spare the world crises and damage that we cannot yet even fathom.[65]

Achievements of the 66th Session

I conclude this chapter by paying tribute to the remarkable achievements of the United Nations member states during the 66th session. It was my great honor to lead the Assembly at a crucial moment in world history. Many times during my term as PGA, it felt that the international community was being tested.

From the historic shifts taking place across the Middle East and North Africa, through a struggling global economic recovery, to   his-toric opportunity to build a more sustainable world—the UN . General Assembly have been called on to act urgently. And in th.   ... of shifting sands, the Assembly has stood strong, active, and responsive. It has built bridges where others may have seen only turbulent waters. It has put aside politics and produced unity, to offer urgent help and hope to those who are most in need.[66]

During the 66th session, the Assembly acted in concert on many of the major issues of our time and adopted around three hundred resolutions and decisions in total.

On Libya, the Assembly restored the legitimate representation of the Libyan people to the General Assembly and the Human Rights Council. This was one of the proudest moments of my term. The Libyan opposition—the National Transitional Council (NTC)—had been trying to raise a voice at the UN, but Muammar Gaddafi's government was still the official representative. (As the host country, the United States is required to grant a certain minimum number of visas to diplomats from all member states.)

I called on the Credentials Committee to challenge the Gaddafi regime's representation. The nine-member Credentials Committee examines the credentials of representatives of member states and reports to the Assembly on those credentials. It is appointed by the Assembly at the beginning of each session on the proposal of the president. The credentials of representatives and the names of members of the delegation of each member state are submitted to the secretary-general and are issued either by the head of state or government or by the minister for foreign affairs.[67] The Credentials Committee decided to replace the Gaddafi regime's delegates with those of the NTC.

That afternoon, the General Assembly endorsed the decision of the Credentials Committee and admitted the NTC's delegates. I invited the NTC representative to take the seat vacated by Gaddafi's delegate. Three days later, the new flag of Libya was raised inside the UN with forty heads of state and government attending, including President Barack Obama and the secretary-general.

The international community is now responding to the aspirations of a new, free Libya. I myself made a joint visit to Libya with the secretary-general on November 2, 2011, to demonstrate the UN's strong support for the Libyans as they embark on this critical journey of reconciliation, democracy, and reconstruction.

On Syria, the General Assembly expressed its concern regarding the ongoing developments in the country. On December 19, 2011, the Assembly adopted a resolution condemning the continued grave and systematic human rights violations committed by the Syrian authorities and calling on them to implement the League of Arab States' Plan of Action in its entirety.[68] We can only hope that the killing and violence in Syria will soon come to an end in keeping with the calls of the international community.

On November 29, 2011, many member states and I reaffirmed our solidarity with the Palestinian people. A number of important resolutions on Palestine were examined by several committees and adopted once again during the 66th session. It is my conviction that the General Assembly should continue to work collectively for the attainment of a just and comprehensive negotiated peace settlement in the Middle East. I would also note here that the Israeli construction of settlements in the occupied Palestinian Territory and the occupied Syrian Golan is of particular concern. I would urge the government of Israel to freeze all settlement activity, as it contravenes international law and the Roadmap.

In keeping with the four pillars I outlined, enormous efforts were made during the 66th session. I would like to highlight some particularly notable achievements.

The first pillar, the peaceful settlement of disputes, reflects my firm belief in the role of mediation to resolve conflicts. To assist with moving this issue forward, I organized a fruitful dialogue called "United Nations Mediation: Experiences and Reflections from the Field" on November 9, 2011. I invite you to consider the summary from this event and to benefit from the valuable lessons shared.[69]

In a related context, I addressed the Fourth Forum of the United Nations Alliance of Civilizations in Doha, Qatar, on December 11, 2011, reiterating the need for youth participation in efforts to advance cross-cultural understanding and sustainable development. More than two thousand participants, including political and corporate leaders, civil society activists, youth groups, faith communities, research centers, foundations, and journalists, came together to agree on joint actions to improve relations across cultures, to combat prejudice, and to build lasting peace.[70] As a follow-up to the Doha forum, in March 2012, I also organized an interactive debate on fostering cross-cultural understanding for building peaceful and inclusive societies. Special attention was given to the role of youth.

The General Assembly, reaffirming its commitment to follow up on the Declaration and Programme of Action on a Culture of Peace, adopted by consensus a resolution emphasizing the need for its full and effective implementation.[71] I call on governments, the secretary-general, and civil society to actively implement this important Declaration and Programme of Action, thereby demonstrating commitment to the promotion of tolerance and nonviolence.

Related to my second pillar, UN reform and revitalization, the formal debate on revitalizing the work of the General Assembly was held on December 1, 2011. Here, the membership reflected its desire for and commitment to a strengthened, responsive, more efficient, and effective General Assembly.

Under my third pillar, improving humanitarian prevention and response, there is no doubt that a consolidation of efforts is required to address more frequent and intense natural disasters, such as we have recently seen in Haiti, Pakistan, Japan, Turkey, Thailand, and the Philippines.

Urgent support is needed in Somalia to protect starving populations that are facing indescribable humanitarian disaster. After proposing a trip at one of my monthly lunches with the secretary-general, I undertook a joint visit to Somalia with him on December 9, 2011. For years, the international community had not paid enough attention to the devastating situation there. During my years as permanent representative, I had pushed hard in the Security Council to put Somalia on the agenda and then presided over a committee on the issue.

A secretary-general and president of the General Assembly had rarely traveled anywhere together, and Ban Ki-moon was understandably concerned that it would not be safe for us to go there; but we agreed that our joint visit could have a real impact. We met in Nairobi, with the secretary-general arriving from a climate-change summit in South Africa. As we were reviewing our plans, the chief of security entered the room to let us know that our itinerary had been leaked. The Boeing 737 that had been loaned to us by Qatar for our travel would be an easy target. We were advised to postpone the trip for our own safety.

I knew that delaying the visit would send a very negative message that would only create more problems in a country that sorely needed our support. I suggested to the secretary-general and our security that we arrive earlier than anticipated, and this is what we did. We hired a less conspicuous propeller plane to fly us to Mogadishu, and then traveling in an armored convoy with African Union troops as well as UN security, we made our way to the president's office at "Villa Somalia."

We reiterated to Somali government officials that the implementation of the Roadmap adopted last September is the way forward. The visit reaffirmed that the UN and the international community stand behind the people of Somalia in the tremendous challenges they face. As a result, several member states opened embassies there. Financial commitments were renewed. The visit also showed how a PGA and the secretary-general, working together, could enhance the visibility and effectiveness of the United Nations. Our traveling together set a precedent that I hope will be followed by future PGAs and secretary-generals.

Great strides have been made under my fourth pillar, sustainable development and global prosperity. In September 2011, the first-ever high-level meeting on desertification was held. It was followed in October by the Conference of the Parties to the UN Convention to Combat Desertification in the Republic of Korea, which I addressed and presented with the high-level meeting summary. At both events, world leaders stressed that desertification is not only harming people but also harming our development and our future and that addressing desertification is an issue of high priority.

We have also had a number of meetings and briefings on sustainable development. In Durban, member states agreed to work toward a new global treaty. Member states also participated in the second dialogue between the General Assembly and the secretary-general's High-Level Panel on Global Sustainability, the briefing on sustainable energy for all, and an informal interactive briefing in preparation for consideration of the secretary-general's annual report on accelerating progress toward the MDGs post-2015.

Turning to macroeconomic issues, given the General Assembly's pre-eminence as the legitimate center of global decision-making, I convened pre- and post-G20 Summit briefings. Here, I encouraged all major groups to cooperate in addressing the challenges of the international economic and financial system. The Assembly also held its fifth High-Level Dialogue on Financing for Development.

At the Global South-South Development Expo in Rome, I reiterated my conviction that South-South and triangular cooperation, backed by adequate funding, are key tools for tackling the development challenges of our time.

In addition to work under these four pillars, significant progress was made in other areas as well, including the following:

Disarmament, in particular nuclear disarmament, remained high on the 66th session agenda. Revitalization of the disarmament machinery, including the Conference on Disarmament in Geneva, is a key requirement for advancing this goal. First committee delegations had a very intensive and constructive exchange on these topics. Accordingly, I visited the Conference on Disarmament in May 2012 and delivered remarks on the occasion of the opening of the second part of their 2012 session.

The political will expressed at the High-Level Meeting on the Prevention and Control of Non-communicable Diseases in September 2011 was a major breakthrough by the international community in protecting the world's most vulnerable populations. I call on all partners to work closely with the World Health Organization to ensure the implementation of the political declaration and will continue to support this any way that I can.

At the commemoration of the tenth anniversary of the adoption of the Durban Declaration and Programme of Action, the political declaration, adopted by consensus, reaffirmed our collective commitment to prevent, combat, and eradicate racism, racial discrimination, xenophobia, and related intolerance.

By adopting resolution 66/10, we welcomed the recent establishment of the United Nations Counter-Terrorism Center at UN Headquarters.[72] I encouraged all member states to collaborate with the center in contributing to the implementation of its activities in support of the United Nations Global Counter-Terrorism Strategy.

Also this session, in the context of the tenth anniversary of the International Year of Volunteers on December 5, 2011, we celebrated the contributions of millions of men and women who selflessly dedicate their time, knowledge, and energy to supporting UN goals and promoting a better world.

Finally, during our memorial service on November 21, 2011, we gathered at UN Headquarters to pay tribute and honor the memory of 197 brave and beloved friends and colleagues who we had recently lost. I underscored again that the safety and security of UN personnel, civilian and uniformed, must be a top priority for the UN and us all.[73]

The Path Ahead

When I ponder the vast agenda of the United Nations, I see the world as it is today but also as it might be tomorrow. I see our hopes, our dreams. I also see all the obstacles that can stand in the way of collective harmony and true peace. And often, I must confess, humility overcomes me, in the face of these daunting challenges.

But history, as Machiavelli vividly tells in the conclusion of his superb treatise *The Prince*, governs only 50 percent of our destiny. The other 50 percent remains in our power, in our *virtu*.[74] Call it "wisdom" or, as we say in Arabic, *barraka*. Whatever name we give it, it is ours if we are lucky and wise enough to act to prevent violence and chaos from engulfing us all in destruction, if we are astute enough to think about the challenges of tomorrow and to deal with them today, if we can rise together and feel that we have contributed something positive to humankind's magnificent journey.[75]

I endeavored, as president of the 66th session, to chart a clear course between idealism and realism. I sought to galvanize the support of member states in building a truly united global partnership on all the important issues we have to address. And the General Assembly, through its actions, reaffirmed its place as the most legitimate, representative, universal body in the world.[76]

It would be both foolish and insincere, however, for scholars and diplomats alike to ignore our collective failure—yes, failure: today in the Middle East, Africa, and other corners of our small world; yesterday in Rwanda and Bosnia.

It would be lacking in intellectual and moral honesty to pretend that the ideals of the UN Charter and of the Universal Declaration of Human Rights have been fully realized. For I have seen firsthand the legacy of brutality imposed by a dictator on his own people in Libya. I have seen the devastating suffering of a whole nation in a Somalia caught in the grinding of competing claims by political factions.

We cannot forget Syria. The conditions in Syria are horrendous. The violence and killing of innocent civilians is ongoing, despite the genuine efforts of the UN and the international community to help bring peace, security, and order to Syria. I am convinced that the international community is mindful of its responsibility to act firmly through the UN to protect the Syrians. We need honest and sincere engagement and a results-oriented plan.

We must move promptly and take action. The lives of tens of thousands of Syrians, and the stability of the region, are at stake. At stake as well is the credibility of the United Nations. I hope that with unity of purpose the United Nations can succeed in helping the people of Syria to resolve this crisis.[77]

Being a witness to our world's continuous tragedies—this is for me a daily lesson of humility and a lucid acknowledgment of the challenges on the road ahead. But it is also a lesson of hope.

Why hope? As a father of a young son, I have no other choice but to hope for a better world—better for him and for all God's children—a world perhaps brought closer to achieving the shared values embodied in the UN Charter and the Universal Declaration of Human Rights.[78]

During my term as PGA, the world welcomed its seven billionth inhabitant. Only by working together can we, the people and nations of the world, ensure that all of Earth's inhabitants—present and future—enjoy the social, economic, and natural conditions conducive to free, productive, and fulfilling lives.[79]

Let us resolve to make it our daily business to work for the advent of that better world. Let us commit ourselves to work together to achieve the universal good.[80]

2

The Peaceful Settlement of Disputes

The Gathering Momentum for Mediation

We live in uncertain times. Unprecedented shifts are taking place across the world. As nations are transforming into new democracies, the moment for mediation is now. Mediation can prevent conflict and stave off bloodshed. Mediation can support peaceful transitions and nurture reconciliation. Mediation is inclusive and can help build representative, democratic societies that realize the legitimate aspirations of their peoples.

In the past, the United Nations has initiated, undertaken, or been involved in several important mediation efforts, either through the good offices of the secretary-general or special representatives and envoys. Examples of successful United Nations mediation include the 1988 cease-fire that ended hostilities in the Iran-Iraq War, the 1988 agreement leading to the withdrawal of Soviet troops in Afghanistan, the 1991 Paris Peace Accords that brought an end to the longstanding conflict in Cambodia, the 1992 agreements that helped end the decade-long civil war in El Salvador, the 1996 settlement that ended three decades of civil war in Guatemala, and the 1999 agreement that led to the independence of Timor-Leste.

In recent years, more and more member states from varied parts of the world have become actively engaged in mediation efforts. Member states are using mediation as a tool to build bridges, settle disputes, and resolve conflicts.[1]

On June 22, 2011—the very same day I was elected president of the General Assembly—the Assembly adopted resolution 65/283, its first-ever resolution on mediation.[2] As permanent representative of Qatar to the United Nations, I had closely followed and contributed to this draft resolution along with my team.[3] (In some cases, multiple resolutions are drafted and submitted by different regional groups; in others, the president coordinates negotiations among regional groups to produce one draft resolution.)[4]

The resolution was a landmark achievement not only for the General Assembly but also for the whole United Nations system. It provides a comprehensive normative framework for UN mediation efforts. The intensive negotiation process for the finalization of this text has itself proven to be very useful in our understanding of almost all aspects of mediation.

The Security Council has also been giving particular emphasis to the matter of mediation over the past few years. On September 22, 2011, the Council held a meeting, under the presidency of Lebanon, on preventive diplomacy. This meeting followed the open debate in July 2011 and the summit in September 2010 on similar issues, after which presidential statements were adopted, pledging to continue strengthening UN capabilities in preventive diplomacy, peacemaking, peacekeeping, and peace building.[5] The 2010 summit was attended by nine heads of state and government as well as six ministers.[6]

The interest of both the General Assembly and the Security Council in mediation is no surprise, because mediation and other peaceful tools are at the very heart of the United Nations. The world is going through a particularly difficult time and transition, and the United Nations can, and should, play an important role in resolving disputes and conflicts worldwide.

Over the past decade, we have also witnessed regional and sub-regional actors, civil society, high-level personalities, women mediators, and elders playing an increasing role by using mediation to prevent and resolve conflicts in various parts of the world. The involvement of these "track II" actors is a welcome trend; however, we have seen that even in such situations, the support of the United Nations was still necessary.

The United Nations has a comparative advantage. It provides international legitimacy to a specific mediation process. Thanks to the recent efforts by the secretary-general to strengthen the United Nations' mediation capacity, the UN system is now supporting member states and other actors in a more effective manner through its able staff, equipped with broad expertise.[7]

The UN's commitment to peacefully resolving disputes is also reflected in the creation of the Advisory Board of the Special Human Settlements Programme for the Palestinian People. The resolution establishing the Advisory Board was drafted by a committee that included Palestine, Israel, Jordan, the United States, Chile, and Rwanda. It is significant that such a wide array of important international actors, including key players on the issue of Palestine, could come together to take this very positive step. I hope that this may serve as a seed for similar initiatives in the future, with a view to improving the living conditions of all peoples in the Middle East and in particular of the Palestinians. Furthermore, such instances of collaboration can also help build trust among the parties and, thus, have positive effects on the wider peace process.[8]

Clearly, the UN is placing increasing emphasis on mediation in the Middle East and around the world. Now, the challenge before us is to keep building this tremendous momentum and further enhance the critical role of mediation in conflict prevention and resolution. It is an issue close to my heart and one which has now become more relevant than ever.

For this reason, I designated the peaceful settlement of disputes as one of the four pillars of my presidency and suggested the theme "The Role of Mediation in the Settlement of Disputes" for the General Debate of the 66th session.[9] I was humbled and encouraged by the strong support expressed by world leaders throughout the debate. Leaders shared their own experiences and approaches to mediation and suggested some useful ideas.

Following the General Debate in September, I organized an interactive meeting with the theme "United Nations Mediation: Experiences and Reflections from the Field" on November 9, 2011. It was attended by former and current high-level UN officials who have led or taken part in mediation processes in different parts of the world, as well as by member states and observers, nongovernmental organizations, and academia. The discussions considered different aspects of the United Nations' role in mediation and contributed to developing guidance on more effective mediation.[10]

We were able to thoroughly discuss the role of the United Nations in mediation and to collect UN-wide experiences from the prevention, peacemaking, and peacekeeping perspectives. We considered questions and challenges facing the UN at Headquarters and on the ground. For instance, with the growing number of mediation actors, is the United Nations still the *primus inter pares*? In spite of recent improvements, is our capacity for mediation sufficient, and how can it be further strengthened? What are the lessons learned from past mediation efforts?[11] The panelists' guidance on these matters should provide a useful tool for mediators at various levels. I circulated a summary of the discussions to all member states.

I continued to make mediation a focus of my work as president of the General Assembly, participating in high-level conferences such as the Fourth Forum of the Alliance of Civilizations in Doha, Qatar, in December 2011 and the International Istanbul Conference with the theme "Enhancing Peace through Mediation" in February 2012.

The Friends of Mediation, cochaired by Turkey and Finland, organized another important meeting on January 11, 2012, in New York, on the role of the regional organizations. This was a useful meeting where we heard directly from regional representatives about the challenges and solutions for mediation at the regional level.[12]

On March 22, 2012, the General Assembly's thematic debate on fostering cross-cultural understanding for building peaceful and inclusive societies gathered member states, representatives of civil society, and the academic community to share their experiences and ideas.[13]

On May 23, 2012, we held a high-level meeting of the General Assembly on the role of member states in mediation. This was a productive meeting focusing on the essential elements for successful mediation efforts.

Finally, on May 31, 2012, I attended the Partners Forum of the Alliance of Civilizations in Istanbul, Turkey. The government of Turkey under the leadership of Prime Minister Recep Tayyip Erdoğan has shown strong support for the Alliance since its inception. Holding this forum in Istanbul was also particularly meaningful because that historic and beautiful city, with its ethnic and cultural diversity, has for centuries illustrated the spirit and principles of the Alliance.[14]

These events are discussed in further detail in the sections that follow.

The Role of the Alliance of Civilizations in the Settlement of Disputes

The United Nations was built on the premise that dialogue is the best path to peace—that cultural diversity, freedom of thought, and knowing each other fosters respect, tolerance, and mutual understanding. Historical experience has shown that diversity of cultures leads to diversity of knowledge and ideas. Science, technology, philosophy—all benefit greatly from the sharing of ideas among people of different cultures and backgrounds.

Recognizing the importance of dialogue for peace and development, the UN member states wisely created the United Nations Alliance of Civilizations. The Alliance was established in 2005—a time when grave tensions rooted in cultural differences gripped our world. It was launched under the auspices of Spain and Turkey and with the full support of the General Assembly, which in its resolution 64/14 welcomed the Alliance and expressed support for its work.[15]

I salute the wisdom and expertise of the members of the high-level group that produced the report establishing the Alliance. This is the UN at its best. When a new need arises, the international community steps up.

The institution soon emerged as a new hope for the international community to stem the tide of intolerance and to offer the public a different perspective. Today, 107 member states count themselves among the Group of Friends of the Alliance of Civilizations. I am hopeful that, in the future, the membership of the Group will be universal.

Under the leadership of His Excellency Jorge Sampaio and with the strong support of United Nations Secretary-General Ban Ki-moon, the Alliance of Civilizations has contributed, through its various activities, to a clear shift in the way we consider issues of "us" and "them." In today's interconnected world, we cannot underestimate the power of such a shift.[16]

In the Alliance's short life, it has also mounted a range of innovative projects to improve understanding between peoples across different cultures and to counter the forces that fuel divisions, incitement to hatred, and extremism. Through partnerships with state and nonstate actors, the Alliance is able to facilitate even more projects at the local, national, and international levels. Its many successes are detailed in the annual report of the high representative.[17]

How do we now help the Alliance to accomplish its mission in a world where cultural identities, cultural differences, need not divide us but unite us and serve as a bridge for a more peaceful and tolerant human family?

Women, youth, media, and immigrant groups—these were the four practical themes that the high-level group's report emphasized as particular domains which, at the moment the Alliance was established, required more specific attention in our search for peace through dialogue and harmony. These four groups remain as important today.

The Fourth Forum of the UN Alliance of Civilizations—convened in Doha, Qatar (my home country), in December 2011—went further and linked the focus on those four areas to development. Thus, the forum recognized that without the full contribution of women, the full contribution of youth, the full contribution of the media, and the full contribution of immigrant groups, there can be no true development and therefore there can be no true peace.

But of course, peace cannot be achieved only through development. For the worst in us—the feelings of superiority that lead to exclusion, the intolerance and contempt that lead to hatred and rejection—these sentiments can lead to mayhem and even war. We have seen it happen throughout history, including in modern times; in Cambodia, in Bosnia, in Rwanda, and elsewhere, intolerance has prevailed with tragic consequences.[18]

The events around us are challenging. Consider for example the awakening in the Arab world. While based in the quest for freedom and dignity, the movement and its consequences underscore the urgent need for governments and communities to commit to building a culture of peace and sustainable development.

Acts of intolerance, extremism, and xenophobia—including the horrifying attacks in Norway in July 2011—have occupied the headlines in recent years. We must pay equal attention to efforts to counter these acts in accordance with international law. It is also important to reaffirm that extremism and hatred cannot be associated with any particular religion, belief system, or culture.[19]

Why is today's world again facing heightened challenges stemming from cultural diversity? Why is culture perceived—and sometimes deeply felt—as a source of division, instead of a path to dialogue and human solidarity? Why is the fear of the "other" an easy platform for those whose simplistic philosophy implies a world of mutually exclusive identities? Why has multiculturalism failed and xenophobia risen in some societies? Why are anti-immigration policies receiving increased political support in many nations?

We have entered a world in which these issues will continue to unsettle us unless we make sure that the benefits of globalization are shared in a just and equitable way among all members of the human family. And so today, the work of the Alliance of Civilizations as a tool for peace is more necessary than ever.

If we fail in this mission, culture and identity will become the refuge of all those who are excluded and left behind. We see today instances in which groups, sometimes nations, are withdrawing from the international conversation at a dire cost to their peoples. Ultimately, this withdrawal represents a loss to us all and brings the world to the threshold of war.

It need not be so. Whatever the financial and other costs of mediation, of strengthening the Alliance of Civilizations, this cost is insignificant compared to the cost of conflict and war. Now more than ever, the Alliance needs resources equal to its objectives.

I can also see a role for the Office of the High Representative in appeasing tensions, preventing misunderstandings, and mediating disputes, particularly when they arise from cultural grievances. As PGA, I appealed to member states to strengthen this role. This would add to our toolbox of conflict prevention and resolution at very little cost to the international community.

Through the Alliance of Civilizations and through the Office of the High Representative, we are given a chance to elevate our consideration of issues of peace and security to a high level of universality and, I hope, to a high level of effectiveness.[20] The time is ripe for exploring new means and partnerships that enhance intercultural dialogue and cooperation. I strongly believe that the Alliance can play a major role in providing fresh and innovative ideas to the international community.[21]

In the short and long term, the activities of the Alliance are vital assets for us to invest in, encourage, and support.[22]

Religion and Mediation

Billions of people around the world identify themselves as believers. One is hard-pressed to find any society, culture, or civilization that has not been shaped to some extent by religious values and practices. In today's interconnected yet divided world, it is more important than ever to draw on religion's potential in the promotion of peace and stability.

Each faith has its unique identity, traditions, and practices. At the same time, we recognize and celebrate the values that are shared across religious traditions. These common principles form a common ground that unites us in our rich diversity.

In October 2010, the UN member states adopted a resolution that proposed World Interfaith Harmony Week as an annual event. In doing so, they underscored the centrality of interfaith cooperation as an important condition for building a culture of peace. During World Interfaith Harmony Week, we not only affirm our own traditions but reflect on the qualities and values of the traditions of others. It is this mutual respect and cooperation that will afford us firm building blocks for the establishment of the culture of peace at all levels.

In many instances, religious organizations provide care and basic services to the world's vulnerable communities. These organizations' efforts have long predated the existence of international development cooperation as we know it today. It is important that the United Nations acknowledges the social and moral significance of this work.

In the General Assembly Hall, where nations gather at a common table of dialogue, issues of faith have rarely been discussed in any systematic way. Recently, however, there has been a greater trend toward dialogue with religious and interfaith organizations at the United Nations. I believe this dialogue should be encouraged.

There is not only common ground that binds different religious traditions together but also a common ground on which religions and the United Nations stand, sharing values and principles. This common ground includes respect for human rights as set out in the Universal Declaration of Human Rights, affirmation of the equal value of all human beings, the importance of compassion and service to others, and the universal aspiration for peace.

Faith-based organizations have long worked in partnership with the United Nations, often in areas of great risk or hardship. Just as the broader NGO community has been a loyal and effective partner and ally to member states, faith-based organizations play a valuable role in advancing the UN's goals.

With this understanding, I organized, in partnership with the Alliance of Civilizations, a one-day interactive thematic debate on "fostering cross-cultural understanding for building peaceful and inclusive societies" on March 22, 2012. The debate drew on the fruitful discussions at the Doha forum in December 2011.[23]

We discussed how to build bridges among different cultures and societies. We considered how to promote dialogue and understanding to effectively address the current tensions and challenges. Participants shared their very useful examples, lessons, and approaches from the international, regional, and national levels. The United Nations Alliance of Civilizations prepared a summary of this informal discussion that was made available to member states and other participants.[24]

As former secretary-general Dag Hammarskjold rightly said, "Unless there is a spiritual renaissance, the world will know no peace." In other words, to build world peace, we must first find peace within ourselves. Let us work together to promote respect for diversity, pluralism, justice, and equality, regardless of religion, gender, race, or ethnicity. As members of the human family, we stand on common ground. From that common ground, let us work together for a world at peace.[25]

The Importance of Track II Actors

On February 25, 2012, I spoke at the International Istanbul Conference on the theme "Enhancing Peace through Mediation: New Actors, Fresh Approaches, Bold Initiatives." In recent years, Istanbul has become a center for mediation efforts. Turkey's efforts and focus range from the Arab-Israeli conflict to Afghanistan-Pakistan, from Iraq to Somalia-Eritrea.

I commend Turkey for its decision to establish a Mediation Center in Istanbul, which will complement its ongoing contribution to regional and international peace and security through mediation.

I was pleased that the main focus of the conference was "track II" actors. Track II actors—such as civil society organizations, research institutions, and former high-level personalities—play a growing role in resolving conflicts, building capacities for dialogue, and engaging in postconflict reconstruction. In some cases, track II actors support and contribute to mediation processes. In others, they initiate, lead, and successfully conclude entire processes.

As past experiences have taught us, every conflict and dispute is distinct. Each one requires careful attention and the most appropriate tools. I would also assert that sometimes track II players have a comparative advantage. They often act in a more informal and flexible way than state actors do. For this reason, the United Nations system, regional organizations, and member states should draw more from the expertise of this track. How can we benefit more from each other's capacities and experiences, and how we can more effectively manage our knowledge and coordinate our efforts?

I consider mediation and cross-cultural dialogue as two issues that are closely interlinked. In some cases, we have to depend on the involvement of local religious leaders, elders, or women's organizations to end violence among groups of different faiths or ethnic groups. These actors have significant leverage and authority in local communities. They are the local track II actors.

Our world is going through a challenging period. It is indeed a period of marked transition: all eyes are on the awakening taking place across the Arab world. Tragically, many people have paid the ultimate price for the establishment of an accountable political system that respects the dignity and basic rights of its people.

Libya is a case in point. I visited Libya in November 2011 and saw firsthand the destruction inflicted on women, children, the society in general, and the overall infrastructure of the country. There were multiple mediation efforts in Libya to ensure a peaceful and smooth transition to democracy. None of the proposals or road maps were accepted by the then leadership in Tripoli.

Libya, Syria, and other similar cases have shown very clearly the importance of mediation at earlier stages of the conflicts, to save lives, protect civilians, and maintain stability. There are lessons to be learned, particularly by those who insist on clinging to power against the will of their own people. We should allow more room for mediation before conflicts erupt and situations worsen.[26]

The Essential Elements for Successful Mediation

At the high-level meeting on the role of member states in mediation on May 23, 2012, we sought to identify the main challenges to effectively dealing with regional and international conflicts. We heard from ministers and other eminent mediators and experts about their experiences and about how mediation processes can be more effectively conducted and managed.[27]

It was a lively and fruitful discussion moderated by international relations expert Edward Luck, special adviser to the assistant secretary-general. We were able to thoroughly look into and discuss the role of member states in mediation as well as the importance of coherence and coordination. We heard different cases, each with its own dynamics.

The meeting produced some good ideas and suggestions that could be further evaluated and developed. These included the establishment of a UN Mediation Center in Istanbul, the launch of an initiative for promotion of mediation in the Mediterranean, and the establishment of national coordination groups that would bring together all the main actors in a country.[28]

We also considered the question, what are the essential elements for successful mediation endeavors? The first is strong leadership and coordinated action. In recent years, there has been a proliferation of mediators, in terms of both number and variety. Depending on the situation and nature of the conflict, there are often multiple actors dealing with different dimensions of an issue. For the sake of coordination and efficiency, however, in each specific case there should be one lead mediator or one lead mediation team. This lead should be supported by others where necessary. This way mediators work together, rather than competing.

The second essential element for a successful mediation process is a fine balance between principles and vision. Among other key elements, a mediator should of course be impartial and neutral. This does not mean, however, that he or she should not have a vision for a possible compromise or resolution of the dispute, based on consultations with, and the expectations of, the parties involved.

The third essential element is knowledge. A mediator should have deep knowledge and a sound understanding of the parties, the situation, the history of the conflict, and the relevant cultural values. During negotiations, the core issues and root causes of the conflict should be properly addressed, so that the peace agreement is viable. Mediators should bear in mind that mediation is an ongoing and dynamic process, requiring a long-term approach and a comprehensive but flexible plan.

The fourth essential element is sustainability and inclusiveness. The sustainability of a peace agreement depends largely on whether it is inclusive. In this respect, female leaders and women's organizations play a vital role in garnering the support of their communities for peace processes. To ensure greater inclusiveness, traditional or indigenous mediation mechanisms should be incorporated and combined with official mediation efforts.

These elements can increase the chances that a mediation process will succeed. But let me be frank. Statistics suggest that there are more mediation failures than mediation successes. Rather than allow this to discourage us, we should thoroughly analyze—at political, legal, and academic levels—the reasons for our shortcomings. And we should seriously consider how to reverse these figures, so that mediation is rightfully employed as a meaningful, effective tool.

Improving our response to, and prevention of, conflicts through dialogue should remain our guiding light. The UN has a central role to play in mediation. It provides legitimacy and expertise to mediation processes. Given the recent, increasing demand for UN participation in mediation efforts, the UN's capability should be further strengthened.

Human rights violations, mass atrocities, and other conflicts are going on across the Middle East, Africa, and elsewhere. This moment is a test. The need for effective mediation is great and growing. Let us show the world that the best way forward—that the only way forward—is through the peaceful settlement of disputes.[29]

3

UN Reform and Revitalization

Reforming the Security Council

From the beginning of my presidency, I identified United Nations reform and revitalization among the four pillars that would guide my work during the 66th session. UN reform is a comprehensive process, and Security Council reform lies at its core.

Reforming the Security Council is critical to reforming and revitalizing the United Nations. Consensus among the international community is undeniable on the need to align the Security Council with contemporary world realities—realities that differ significantly from those of May 1945.[1]

For almost two decades, there has been serious discussion within the United Nations' halls on how to achieve this reform. Having followed these discussions for thirteen years as an ambassador to the United Nations, I realize that we have invested serious time discussing the different theoretical foundations of this process.

Different models for reform have emerged, reflecting the views of various groups. The Group of Four (G4)—Brazil, Germany, India, and Japan—argues for six additional permanent seats and four additional nonpermanent seats. Four of the six new permanent seats would be reserved for themselves, while the remaining two would be granted to African states. The G4 has been careful not to raise the issue of veto powers for new permanent members.

The L69 Group proposes six additional permanent seats, including two for Africa and, like the G4, one each for Brazil, Germany, India, and Japan. L69 differs from the G4 proposal by maintaining that all permanent members should have veto powers. In the nonpermanent-member category, the L69 also proposes four additional seats, with one of these seats reserved for a small developing state. The African Union/C10 proposes an increase of six permanent seats, with four going to the G4 and two being reserved for Africa. Regarding the veto, the proposal calls for equal veto powers among new and old permanent member states.

Uniting for Consensus is the only group that does not propose any increase in permanent members. Instead, it proposes an increase of twelve additional nonpermanent members. Flexibility is added to this plan through the creation of semipermanent seats with longer durations, as well as a redistribution of nonpermanent seating by region. Combining the new and existing nonpermanent seats, the proposed regional distribution would grant approximately six seats to Africa, five to Asia, four to Latin America and the Caribbean, one or two to eastern Europe, and three to the "western European and others" group. Uniting for Consensus is adamant in resolving the issue by consensus.

Meanwhile, the Accountability, Coherence and Transparency Group (ACT) seeks to improve the working methods of the Security Council, which should operate in a more transparent, efficient, inclusive, coherent, legitimate, and accountable way, both within its own structure and in relationship with the wider membership.[2] The five permanent members of the Security Council (P5) have a different position on the issue.[3]

Unfortunately, after years of long debate in the General Assembly—whether formally or informally, at the bilateral level or in the wider context of the UN membership—there has not been much actual progress.[4]

In 2005, the UN member states adopted the outcome document of the World Summit, in which we stressed our support "for early reform of the Security Council—as an essential element of our overall effort to reform the United Nations—in order to make it more broadly representative, efficient and transparent and thus to further enhance its effectiveness and the legitimacy and implementation of its decisions." The paragraph continues, "We commit ourselves to continuing our efforts to achieve a decision to this end and request the General Assembly to review progress on the reform set out above by the end of 2005."[5]

Considering these words, the member states must ask ourselves, what is the implication of the current status quo on our organization? Could the failure of the Council to respond to specific challenges erode the credibility of the United Nations?

My honest answer is, yes. Sustaining the central role of the UN in the global arena demands serious progress with regard to Security Council reform.

This leads to my next question: when can we achieve this progress? My answer is again in the spirit of the 2005 document: as soon as possible. Yet with the tenth anniversary of the World Summit quickly approaching, progress has been neither quick nor assured.

Another question I would submit is, what should Security Council reform look like? I believe that our efforts to reform the Council should chart a course between realism and idealism. I stated, as PGA, that I would support any approach that enjoys the widest political acceptance among the UN membership. Member states must drive the process in the manner defined in the General Assembly Decision 62/557.[6]

At the General Debate in September 2011, world leaders reflected on the pressing need for Security Council reform—reform that would make the Council more efficient, transparent, universal, and democratic. On November 8, 2011, we met to consider agenda item 122: the question of equitable representation on—and increase in the membership of—the Security Council.[7] This was followed by an informal dialogue on Security Council reform hosted by the government of Japan on November 14.

At each occasion, I emphasized the need to engage in constructive discussions on the issue of reform with patience and a spirit of compromise. By doing so, we will maximize our opportunities for progress. I believe that the primary responsibility for realizing our aspiration to reform the Security Council lies with the member states.[8]

To that end, I organized a General Assembly retreat at Glen Cove, New York, in March 2012 on the topic of Security Council reform. Member states gathered along with experts from civil society and academia to work and think innovatively together and to discuss how we can proceed with this process. The secretary-general, His Excellency Mr. Ban Ki-moon, was also in attendance, demonstrating his ongoing support of member states on this important issue.[9] The workshop was ably moderated by Ambassador Zahir Tanin, permanent representative of Afghanistan to the UN and chair of the intergovernmental negotiations on Security Council reform. We listened to different views on how to progress, both from within the UN and from outside. Dialogue was thought-provoking, inspiring, and concrete.

Some participants favored expansion of the Council membership in both permanent and nonpermanent categories. Others, including thirty countries known in this context as the "Coffee Club," prefer to increase only the number of nonpermanent members.[10] In the end, what emerged from the discussions was a sincere quest for a results-oriented, future-looking approach. We did not expect to conclude a challenging exercise such as Security Council reform during one General Assembly session. However, we recognized that we must achieve concrete steps forward each session until we reach our goal.

Was the retreat successful? I do believe it was a step in the right direction, having recharged our momentum. But only time will tell. Success will come only from actual results. We need to move forward despite the differing views of member states. The stalemate of the reform process threatens the UN's ability and credibility to undertake its chartered mandate.

In recent years, there have been many urgent issues—from illegal settlements to the situation in Syria—on which the world has looked to the United Nations and particularly to the Security Council in hope of a swift response for the protection of rights, dignity, security, and ultimately lives. Sadly, in some cases, this global hope has not been equally matched by the Council's actions.

The status quo is not an option. I am pleased to say the 66th session was the most engaged session ever on the issue of Security Council reform. From my first day in office, I appointed the ambassador from Afghanistan as the cofacilitator on the issue, and he organized eight informal meetings in addition to the retreat at Glen Cove. Although the essence of the problem remains, I hope that my contributions as president of the General Assembly have better prepared us to continue working toward achieving real reform—reform that is vital to preserving the effectiveness of the United Nations in responding to current challenges.[11] Skeptics outside the system say it is impossible for the UN to fix its own problems. They say that perhaps it will take another world war to achieve real change. But from where I am sitting as a global policymaker, reform is unavoidable, and I firmly believe that the PGA will play a key role in achieving it.

Empowering the General Assembly

The Security Council is not the only body of the United Nations that requires revitalization. More than ever before, events around the world necessitate a strong and responsive General Assembly.

The Assembly is, after all, the UN's chief deliberative, policymaking, and representative organ. It is, I would submit, the most universal, legitimate body in the world. The General Assembly has a tremendous mandate, and we must use it: as the universal place for finding solutions, responding to challenges, and building global consensus.

To meet the current global challenges and to fulfill the General Assembly's central role as envisaged by the UN Charter, the Assembly must be revitalized and empowered. Member states must make joint efforts to ensure the Assembly remains efficient, competent, and viable.

Revitalization of the General Assembly is of course not a new issue. It has been on our agenda since the early 1990s. Discussions to date have embraced different views. Some have focused more on technical and administrative issues, such as how to improve the Assembly's working methods and rationalize its agenda. Others have highlighted the urgent need to revitalize the Assembly's political role and its authority as defined by the UN Charter.[12]

I would argue that one of the most fundamental elements for strengthening the General Assembly and ensuring its effectiveness is the implementation of its own resolutions and decisions. Implementation is the responsibility of the member states. It is their task to translate international commitments into national legislation and policies.[13]

Too many resolutions and decisions adopted by the Assembly are yet to be implemented. The General Assembly should not be restricted to a venue for deliberation. Rather, it is a place for finding solutions, responding to challenges, and building global consensus on issues of shared concern.

To date, we have seen notable developments on a number of fronts. The practice of electing the president of the General Assembly at least three months before he or she takes office, a revision of the rules of procedure adopted in 2002, now enables president-elects to better prepare for the session.[14] Similarly, supporting the prerogative of the president to organize informal thematic debates has brought the Assembly to closely consider contemporary pressing issues of global concern.

Progress is yet to be achieved, however, in areas including the procedure for the nomination of the secretary-general, the working methods of the Assembly, and the implementation of General Assembly resolutions. And while there has been consensus on the need to support the institutional memory of the Office of the President of the General Assembly, I believe that this support should extend to further strengthening the political role of the PGA in the global arena, with particular attention to the president's potential role as a mediator.

It is also worth noting here that the process of General Assembly revitalization falls under the wider umbrella of United Nations reform.[15] In that regard, as PGA, I stressed the importance of cooperation and coordination among the UN's principal organs. (As established in the UN Charter, the six principal organs of the organization are the General Assembly, the Security Council, the Economic and Social Council, the Trusteeship Council, the International Court of Justice, and the Secretariat.)[16]

Genuine efforts have been made in recent years to strengthen the relationship between the General Assembly and the Security Council. During my presidency, I sought to continue, and to accelerate, this process. On November 8, 2011, the then-president of the Security Council, His Excellency Ambassador José Filipe Moraes Cabral, presented the annual Security Council report to the General Assembly.

The annual Security Council report is one of the main instruments for cooperation between the General Assembly and the Security Council. During this particular reporting period, the Security Council had faced tremendous challenges including the postelection crisis in Cote d'Ivoire, the declaration of the state of South Sudan, and a variety of developments in the Arab world, in particular in Libya, Yemen, and Syria.

On issues of tremendous importance such as these, it is crucial that the Security Council and the General Assembly work hand in hand to ensure the success of our organization in its endeavors. As president of the General Assembly, I met with each and every president of the Security Council. (The position rotates monthly.) The presidents of the Security Council and I had intensive and fruitful discussions on how to better coordinate our work and to improve the cooperation between us. Our teams were in constant contact to ensure a smooth conduct in both organs, to prevent conflicting agendas, and to strengthen our joint efforts.[17]

I also held regular interactions with the presidents of the Economic and Social Council, as well as with the Secretariat.[18] The secretary-general, His Excellency Mr. Ban Ki-moon, and I conducted a joint visit to Libya in November 2011 that was quite timely and productive. As discussed in chapter 1, we also visited Somalia together in December 2011 to deliver a message of support for those who were suffering the unbearable hardships caused by the scourge of conflict.

Regarding the situation in Syria, the General Assembly's engagement reflects the very mission of our organization: to keep peace throughout the world and to encourage respect for human rights and freedoms. In February 2012, the Assembly provided a venue for the international community to consider the ongoing human rights situation in Syria, including through a briefing by the high commission for human rights, Navi Pillay, followed by the adoption of resolution 66/253, on February 16.[19] These actions represent practical measures to revitalize the role and effectiveness of the General Assembly.

Reforming the United Nations relies, in large part, on enhancing the role and authority of the General Assembly to let the Assembly attain the political power it deserves and the prestige necessary to reflect its role in global decision-making. Through continued coordination between UN bodies and offices, we shall further strengthen the ability of our organization to undertake its mandate.[20]

Strengthening the Office of the President of the General Assembly

I believe the revitalization of the General Assembly can be further enhanced by empowering its president.

Bearing in mind the Assembly's heavy and growing agenda, it is essential to fully understand the context within which the president of the General Assembly currently undertakes his or her mandate. The PGA spearheads the efforts and the collective responsibility of member states to drive forward the agenda of the Assembly, to lead and facilitate the follow-up processes on substantive mandates, and to help to move forward processes when needed.

Additionally, in order to ensure that the voice of the General Assembly is heard worldwide, the president has the responsibility to conduct outreach on many levels. The Assembly has encouraged such actions by requesting that its presidents increase their public visibility.

The presidents are therefore obliged to broaden the scope of their duties beyond the UN Headquarters in New York and across duty stations such as Geneva, Nairobi, and Vienna in order to reaffirm the Assembly's central role in global governance.

The president's outreach provides assurances, especially to marginalized and vulnerable communities of the world, that the United Nations stands in solidarity with them. The president's briefings to the general membership following such important meetings not only enable member states to remain up-to-date on the most recent developments but also help to bring key messages from far corners of the world to the international community.[21]

The increasing responsibilities of the president of the General Assembly demand an appropriate budget in support of his or her mission. As those readers in the UN system are aware, the president has to search for external budgetary supports, which constitutes an extra burden on the presidency and threatens to expose the office to political influence from funders.

Indeed, if we ensure that the functions of the Office of the President are supported through the UN's biennium budget, then developing and least developed countries would be encouraged to nominate their representatives for the presidency and to contribute their rich expertise at this level.[22]

Furthermore, the president of the General Assembly's challenging mandate normally extends within a period of only one complete session: twelve months. The PGA does not always find this limited period of time appropriate or sufficient for familiarizing him- or herself with the office, while also driving the rich and diversified agenda of the Assembly.

Whether or not the PGA's term is extended, we need to work on strengthening the institutional memory of the office. I have four suggestions for how to achieve this.

First, based on my own experience, it is crucial that adequate time be made for a transition between the presidencies. My team opted to commence our work over a period that overlapped with the tenure of my predecessor. This overlap gave us the opportunity to pick up some useful "best practices" and lessons learned.

Second, we should consider using a "troika" of presidents—that is, the past, present, and incoming PGAs—on occasions when such expertise is needed. I found it helpful during my term to remain in close contact with my predecessors, and I stand ready to provide any assistance and support to future presidents toward maintaining the institutional memory of the office.

Third, proper documentation and archiving of the records of the office are essential. During the 66th session, we undertook a number of measures in this regard, such as revamping and enhancing the PGA's website with more detail on my meetings and participation in international forums. We also maintained thorough electronic archives of the contributions of various specialists to our work and of the general activities of the office.

A competent, professional staff including the speechwriter—a dedicated post provided during the 66th session—as well as the spokesperson and the assistant, has been instrumental in upholding the high standards of communication and transparency of the PGA. Allow me to mention here that the contributions of some member states in the form of secondment of staff, and particularly the immense support of the government of the State of Qatar, went a long way in supporting me to carry out the mandated activities of the office in an effective manner.

Fourth, the retention of some of the core advisers from one session to the next would ensure continuity of functional expertise and thereby enhance the institutional memory of the office.

Effective coordination with the Secretariat and the Security Council was instrumental to the success of my presidency. I also sought strong partnerships with civil society organizations, NGOs, and the private sector on issues of global concern—especially in the areas of inclusive and sustainable development, peace and security, and human rights. I appointed a special coordinator for civil society to facilitate the constructive and meaningful engagement of civil society in accordance with the rules and procedures set by member states. The capacity of the Office of the President to undertake effective and highly beneficial partnership with civil society should be strengthened to ensure continuity and greater benefits.

It is surprising that at a time when the UN's overall budget has grown in every other area, the level of resources allocated to the Office of the President has remained unchanged since 1998–1999. This is especially disappointing in light of the exponential increase in the activities of the office in recent years. Moreover, the trust fund established in support of the office for initiatives such as specific thematic debates did not receive any contributions for the 66th session.

Recognizing the difficult financial situation facing the Office of the President, the General Assembly in its resolution 66/246 on the proposed budget for 2012–2013 has requested the secretary-general to submit proposals to review the resource allocation to the office in the context of the next budget.[23] I also call on member states to contribute generously to the work of the Office of the President in the coming sessions, either through the trust fund, secondments, or voluntary contributions.

I hope that, in order to ensure the independence and effective running of the Office of the President of the General Assembly, the General Assembly will take adequate measures to improve the financial situation of the office. This could be done at least to match the evolution of the regular budget of the organization, including by approving dedicated conference-service resources and additional staff.

The inadequacy of the resources currently available to the office also undermines the president's outreach capacity and therefore constrains effective participation in regional meetings and other international forums. The provision of additional resources to enhance the president's outreach capacity would augur well for current efforts to improve the visibility of the office and the work of the organization at large.

As I conclude this section, I would like to note that as president, I have been careful to build on the progress achieved during previous sessions on a variety of issues. I hope that future presidents will also carry forward the progress we have managed to achieve during the 66th session with the full support of member states.[24]

Enhancing the Role of ECOSOC

A key priority of the 66th session of the General Assembly was to strengthen the UN system for global governance through creative, adaptive structural changes. Emerging challenges to the international system have resulted in suggestions of reform of UN bodies. In particular, serious concerns relating to food security and the current global financial crisis have exposed how fragile and fragmented global economic governance has become. It is very appropriate and in all of our interest for the Economic and Social Council (ECOSOC), in keeping with its UN Charter–mandated responsibility, to assume greater responsibility in this area.

I believe that ECOSOC reform efforts should be an ongoing exercise, taking into account the ever-changing global scene. In this context, reforms should focus on the organization's added value in its role for overall coordination, avoiding duplication with other bodies or the proliferation of meetings.

Strengthening ECOSOC assumed increasing importance during the 66th session as Rio+20, the MDG target year of 2015, and the articulation of the post-2015 development agenda of the UN all converged on the global agenda.

In November 2011, permanent representatives and senior UN officials gathered for a retreat in Manhasset, New York, to explore ways and means of further enhancing ECOSOC's role and effectiveness in addressing the challenges encountered in the area of global economic and social development. Discussion focused on how ECOSOC could respond in a timely and meaningful way to new and emerging concerns.

From my perspective having served in the General Assembly, ECOSOC has a number of opportunities to build on its existing strengths and increase its effectiveness. One area that requires attention is ECOSOC's relationships with intergovernmental organizations. ECOSOC's effectiveness will be further constrained if it does not engage strategically with these existing and emerging institutions.

Another relevant area is the relationship between ECOSOC and the Bretton Woods institutions (the World Bank and International Monetary Fund). The United Nations Charter stipulates in Articles 57 and 63 that the specialized agencies (including the Bretton Woods institutions) "shall be brought into relationship" with the United Nations by entering into agreements to define the terms of the relationship and that the United Nations Economic and Social Council (ECOSOC) "may coordinate the activities of the specialized agencies through consultation with and recommendations to such agencies."

In ECOSOC, each country has one vote, while in the Bretton Woods institutions there is "weighted voting" on the basis of a country's shares. In addition, ECOSOC is largely a policymaking organ, while the World Bank Group provides some $52.6 billion to more than eighteen hundred projects in developing countries, together with financial and technical expertise. Since 2003, an annual high-level meeting between ECOSOC and the Bretton Woods institutions (also attended by the World Trade Organization and the United Nations Conference on Trade and Development) has brought together ECOSOC and the Bretton Woods institutions to increase coordination and synergy. We need to build on earlier successes in improving their cooperation and coherence on global economic and financial matters and in bolstering ECOSOC's identity as the "port of entry" for discussions on these issues.

Recognizing that peace and development are two sides of the same coin, it is encouraging that ECOSOC intends to focus on the links between peace, security, and development. I hope that these gaps in global economic governance—and strategies for ECOSOC to overcome them—will remain a priority of the organization and that ECOSOC will continue to enjoy the full support of the General Assembly. Only by revitalizing the entire United Nations system can we ensure that today's UN is equipped to address the new global realities.[25]

4

Natural Disaster Prevention and Response

The UN's Role in Disaster Prevention and Response

In recent years, many countries—Haiti, Pakistan, Japan, Turkey, and the United States, among others—have been struck by major natural disasters. It is clear that Mother Nature does not discriminate between rich and poor nations. In many of the affected countries, the loss of human life has been staggering, and sources of livelihood have been almost totally wiped out. The relationship between disasters and the rise in poverty is perfectly clear, and what is more, scientists are predicting an increase in natural disasters in the years to come.

Meanwhile, the financial, social, and political costs of such disasters are steadily increasing. In 2010 alone, the world witnessed more than 347 natural disasters, tragically impacting over 255 million people. More than 100,000 human lives were lost, and the economic cost has been estimated at over US$304 billion. These natural disasters are a sober reminder to the international community of the importance of prioritizing disaster preparedness and ensuring effective disaster recovery.

Less visible but similarly devastating is the severe lack of water for agriculture and production in arid areas where people can no longer earn a living. The economic losses from such situations are relentlessly increasing. The social and economic damage on development is considerable.

As the president of the 66th session of the General Assembly, I made prevention and reduction of the impact of disasters one of the four pillars of my service. Underpinning this focus was the recognition that humanitarian issues are development issues, and success in protecting against natural disasters, such as extreme drought, will have a direct impact on our ability to fulfill the MDGs.

During my term, our work in disaster prevention and relief focused on the crisis in Somalia and the Horn of Africa, which is described in further detail in the next section. Though significant improvements in the situation have been achieved, much work remains to be done.

As in other areas of focus, the UN can be most effective in its efforts to respond to natural disasters when it works in coordination with other organizations. I welcome and congratulate the initiative of the Arab Aid Consortium as major donors to infrastructural, social, and economic development and capacity building and training and their commitment to integrating the perspective of risk reduction in practice. This is of great importance to the Arab region as well as for all countries worldwide.[1]

The Humanitarian Crisis in the Horn of Africa

Men, women, and children in the Horn of Africa are facing starvation and humanitarian disaster on an unimaginable scale. As the world's preeminent forum for international peace and security, the UN has the responsibility to provide moral and financial support to these highly vulnerable populations. The rights to food, life, and security are, after all, universal human rights.

On September 24, 2011, the General Assembly held a Mini-Summit on the Humanitarian Crisis in the Horn of Africa. World leaders emphasized the need to combat desertification and its severe humanitarian consequences.

The solidarity demonstrated by countries from around the world on this issue illustrates the ability and willingness of the international community to respond when people are in dire need. I welcome all the resources that have been mobilized, and in particular I would like to recognize regional initiatives, especially those of the African Union and the Organization of the Islamic Conference, whereby countries have come together to help their neighbors.

Going forward, the effectiveness of these contributions will depend on the ability of governments and humanitarian organizations to act in concert in the Horn of Africa, particularly in Somalia. I would encourage member states to use the multilateral assistance framework, or work closely with it, to ensure that their generous contributions are effectively used to save lives and to help rebuild local resilience.

It is also important that bilateral aid is coordinated with the UN system, through the Emergency Relief Coordinator, United Nations Office for the Coordination of Humanitarian Affairs, to ensure the sustainability of current donations and investments. In the longer term, it will be important to support national efforts that improve communities' resilience and self-reliance in responding to increasingly recurrent droughts.

During the 66th session, the resolution on strengthening humanitarian assistance in the Horn of Africa provided an important opportunity for member states to clearly delineate their commitment to addressing this unfolding crisis. The resolution will also help the affected member states to reinforce their ability to avert another famine. Adoption of this resolution was an important step in responding to the crisis. It also demonstrated the General Assembly's quick response to emerging situations of global concern.[2]

On December 21, 2011, I convened a meeting to brief the General Assembly on the joint official visit that I made with UN Secretary-General Ban Ki-moon to Somalia on December 9. The secretary-general and I felt that it was very important to visit the country, to demonstrate that the United Nations stands with the Somalis at this critical moment.

For more than two decades, the people of Somalia have been going through a very painful and difficult period of violence, conflict, and civil strife, which has claimed the lives of many civilians. Somalis have experienced untold suffering and severe devastation of their country's resources. During the summer of 2011, the humanitarian situation rapidly deteriorated. Famine was declared in six areas of Somalia.

In June 2011, the Kampala Accord was signed between Somalia's president and its speaker of parliament. In August, the insurgents of Al-Shabaab were forced to withdraw from the capital. The following month, in September, the Transitional Federal Government (TFG) and its partners agreed on an inclusive Roadmap for ending the transition. The Roadmap includes finalization and adoption of the constitution, parliamentary reform, and improvements in governance and security.

The African Union Mission in Somalia (AMISOM) is continuing to consolidate its control over the capital, and Kenya is also on board to support the Transitional Federal Government. Since October 2011, there has been a slight sign of improvement in the situation in Somalia due to increased humanitarian assistance. Three of the country's six regions were lifted out of famine in mid-November 2011 thanks to the efforts of international and local aid workers on the ground.

The improvement created a window of opportunity to promote national reconciliation and inclusive political processes. In Mogadishu, Secretary-General Ban and I held meetings with His Excellency President Sheikh Sharif Sheikh Ahmed; His Excellency Dr. Adiweli Mohamed Ali, Prime Minister of the Transitional Federal Government; and His Excellency Sharif Hassan Sheikh, Speaker of the Transitional Federal Parliament. We discussed a wide range of issues including the humanitarian and security situations and the implementation of the Somali Roadmap.

As president of the General Assembly and on behalf of the member states of the United Nations, I extended to the government and the people of Somalia my commitment to help ensure a better, safer, and more prosperous tomorrow. We urged the Somali authorities to provide exemplary leadership and to intensify efforts to promote full national reconciliation. We encouraged them to abide by their commitment to complete the transitional tasks set out by the Roadmap and made it clear that while the United Nations and the international community stand ready to offer whatever assistance they can, it is ultimately up to the Somalis to determine whether the Roadmap succeeds.

The secretary-general and I then visited the Dadaab refugee complex in Kenya, which is the largest one providing shelters for Somali refugees. We extended our gratitude to the government of Kenya for its generous support. We were deeply saddened by the suffering of the refugees. In order to assess the impact of famine and disease in the region, I was accompanied by my senior adviser on humanitarian and public health, a physician who has been conducting medical research and relief work in the Horn of Africa for many decades.

During our meeting with international and local aid workers there, I commended their life-saving work on the ground. I stressed that their security and safety is also a top priority. I also commended the efforts made by AMISOM and its steadfast commitment to peace in Somalia, as well as the efforts by the United Nations high commissioner for refugees, the Office for the Coordination of Humanitarian Assistance, and all other UN personnel and civil society members. Each of their staffs is doing an extraordinary job trying to save lives and to help build local capacities. It is important to stress here, though, that they must be able to continue to perform their missions unhampered. I urge all parties to respect humanitarian law.

The special representative of the secretary-general, Mr. Augustine P. Mahiga, is leading with great professionalism. I welcomed the secretary-general's announcement that the UN Political Office for Somalia (UNPOS) led by Mahiga and his core team would—after a seventeen-year absence—be relocating to Mogadishu the following month. I extended all my support to Mahiga and his office, as well as the entire UN country team working closely to support the TFG's efforts in governance, recovery, development, and capacity building.[3]

Despite the improvements witnessed on our trip, the security situation in Somalia remained challenging. In June 2012, the secretary-general and I attended the second Istanbul Conference on Somalia, with the theme "Preparing Somalia's Future: Goals for 2015."

The conference aimed to map concrete actions in the political, security, and economic spheres that would ensure a smooth end to the transition and help establish an inclusive and broad-based political framework in Somalia. Leadership of the Somali authorities is key to intensifying efforts to promote full national reconciliation. I encouraged them to abide by their commitment of the London Somali Conference, to complete the transitional tasks by the end of the extended transitional period, on August 20, 2012.

While the international community stands ready to offer assistance and investment, the success of the Roadmap is ultimately up to Somalis. It is essential to set up a constituent assembly that is inclusive and transparent. Somalia's new interim constitution should reflect the aspirations and expectations of the Somali people, as well as the fundamental principles of human rights.

The African Union Mission to Somalia (AMISOM) has made steady progress, and the deployment beyond Mogadishu was critical and a very positive step. In implementation of resolution 2036 adopted by the Security Council in February 2012, AMISOM capacities will be reinforced.[4] However, more support is necessary to finance AMISOM stipends.

We still face many challenges. There are continued, widespread, grave violations of international humanitarian and human rights law, especially against the most vulnerable. Here, I must mention the crisis of piracy, which has been addressed by the General Assembly. I would also note that targeting, obstructing, or preventing the delivery of humanitarian aid, and any attack on humanitarian personnel, is unacceptable.

The second Istanbul Conference provided an opportunity to reaffirm our commitment to Somalia, but the humanitarian situation asks for continued attention. Let us all join our efforts to achieve peace for Somalia and the Horn of Africa.[5]

The HOPEFOR Initiative

In November 2011, the State of Qatar hosted the first International Conference on the HOPEFOR initiative: improving the effectiveness and coordination of military and civil defense assets for natural disaster response. The intensive work of Qatar in this regard is indicative of its active involvement in the work of the United Nations.

The conference offered a rich and substantive dialogue. Our experience and lessons learned over the past decades have demonstrated that the effective use of military and civilian assets for natural disaster response can make a real difference on the ground, owing to the possibilities such use offers for saving lives and minimizing the impact of disasters. Indeed, disasters can sometimes exceed the capacities of humanitarian organizations.

Inevitably, this raises questions about the modalities and conditions of the use of military assets. The primary responsibility for responding to a disaster rests, of course, with the affected state. Accordingly, its consent, with respect to its sovereignty, is an essential prerequisite for the delivery of such assistance by outside parties, in accordance with international law, including international humanitarian law and other relevant statutory instruments.

The function of civilian and military defense assistance must always be to supplement existing relief mechanisms. Furthermore, military humanitarian operations must also respect established guidelines to ensure impartiality, neutrality, humanity, and independence from political considerations. Herein lies the importance of the HOPEFOR initiative, which aims to address existing gaps in the use of military and civilian assets; to develop improved civilian-military coordination in humanitarian operations; to ensure that military and civilian assets in disaster-relief operations are appropriate, effective, and coordinated; and to support the existing United Nations humanitarian emergency response system.

To crown the tireless efforts of the State of Qatar, the Dominican Republic, and the Republic of Turkey, the General Assembly of the United Nations, adopted, by consensus, resolution 65/307, "Improving the Effectiveness and Coordination of Military and Civil Defense Assets for Natural Disaster Response."[6] I personally attended to the draft resolution during my term as permanent representative of the State of Qatar to the United Nations.

In adopting this resolution, the international community recognized, first, that building national and local preparedness and response capacity is critical to a more predictable and effective response; second, that it is important to promote preparedness for disaster response through regional and international partnerships; and third, that while humanitarian assistance is fundamentally civilian in character, there is a need to support military involvement and assets in situations where they can play an important role.

The United Nations system, and the Office for the Coordination of Humanitarian Affairs in particular, is already making a significant difference in providing humanitarian relief and rescue services. The purpose of the HOPEFOR initiative is to provide support for, not to replace, the important work of humanitarian agencies. It also seeks to supplement the United Nations system in disaster risk reduction and prevention activities. In addition, the initiative emphasizes the need for concrete measures such as the establishment of a global network of civilian and military practitioners and the establishment of the Centre of Excellence in Doha to coordinate the use of military and civil defense assets for natural disaster response.

In closing this chapter, I would like to reiterate that the experience of recent years has shown that investment in disaster risk prevention can save many lives. The life of a human being is infinitely valuable, and defending it is something that unites us all. Consequently, it is incumbent on us to adapt our capacities so as to be able to deal with the forces of nature. Progress in this domain depends on effective partnerships; we must work together to meet this global challenge. As president of the General Assembly and today as high representative for the Alliance of Civilizations, I have remained firmly committed to pursuing more effective disaster risk reduction and enhanced international responsiveness.[7]

5

Sustainable Development and Global Prosperity

Supporting Sustainable Development

The fourth and final of the key areas I focused on as president of the General Assembly was sustainable development and global prosperity. Dramatic changes are occurring across the globe. The volatility of food and energy prices threatens millions of poor people with still deeper poverty. Extreme weather and other impacts of climate change continue to jeopardize development gains. Taken in combination, these factors affect our well-being and feed anxiety about the future—our own and that of our children.[1]

During the 66th session, we marked a historic milestone in human development: seven billion people living on this planet. Seven billion people now depend on governments, civil society, the private sector, and the international community at large to ensure their development and to protect and promote their human rights. Seven billion people now face the consequences of environmental challenges, increasing poverty, inequity, wars, and economic instability. The poorest billion are extremely vulnerable, with little or no access to basic needs.

But with each of these challenges comes an opportunity—seven billion opportunities in fact: to come together and provide where there is need; to reach the MDGs; to rethink our approach to sustainable development in the face of increasing pressure on our communities and on our environment; to pool our collective financial, moral, and human capital; to replicate, adjust, and realize where there are successful solutions; to appreciate, recognize, and share in the wealth of our diversity, knowing that discrimination and intolerance have no place in our world; to invest in youth and in women; to work together to ensure that national policies and international cooperation in the field of financing for development promote the creation of productive employment; and to showcase the UN's ability to deliver as one.[2]

In 1992, by adopting Agenda 21, world leaders at the Earth Summit set out the principles of sustainable development and highlighted that no one nation can achieve sustainable development alone. Its recommendations ranged from new ways to educate to new ways to care for natural resources and new ways to participate in designing a sustainable economy.[3] Over the past twenty years, governments, businesses, and civil society have accepted this paradigm as imperative for making progress on the three pillars of sustainable development: economic, social, and environmental.

Implementation has proven difficult, and many commitments remain largely unfulfilled. As PGA, I worked to provide the appropriate settings for member states to exchange lessons learned, to bridge the gaps, and to build consensus leading up to the twentieth anniversary of the Earth Summit (Rio+20).[4] The conference presented an important benchmark in the global development agenda and global strategy for sustainable development. Rio+20 sought to address gaps in means of implementation, the green economy in the context of poverty eradication, and the strengthening of the institutional framework for sustainable development.[5]

I participated in a number of other important global conferences on sustainable development during my term as PGA. In October 2011, the international community met in Changwon City, Republic of Korea, at the tenth session of the Conference of the Parties of the UN Convention to Combat Desertification (UNCCD COP10).[6] There I delivered the report of the high-level meeting on desertification, which the General Assembly held in September. The conference adopted forty decisions, including ones addressing the governance of the UNCCD's Global Mechanism, scientific advice, and performance and impact indicators.[7]

Another key meeting was UNCTAD13, the United Nations Conference on Trade and Development event from April 21 to 26 in Doha, Qatar, with the theme "Development-Centred Globalization: Towards Inclusive and Sustainable Growth and Development." Since UNCTAD's creation in 1964, the Geneva-based institution has been the one that has best translated the struggle and aspirations of developing countries for expanding trade and for developing their capacities and potential. It promotes the integration of developing countries into the world economy. It functions as a forum for intergovernmental deliberations; it undertakes research, policy analysis, and data collection for the debates of government representatives and experts; and it provides technical assistance tailored to the requirements of developing countries, with special attention to the needs of the least developed countries and of economies in transition.[8]

As the first major United Nations ministerial conference on trade and development since the beginning of the economic crisis, UNCTAD13 provided an opportunity for much-needed reflection on the impact of the crisis on trade and development, in particular for developing countries.[9]

The results of these conferences and other important events are discussed in greater detail in the remaining sections of this chapter. I would like to acknowledge here that before taking office as the president of the General Assembly, I was deeply involved in development issues in my capacity as the ambassador and permanent representative of Qatar to the United Nations. Naturally, I am proud of my country's significant contributions to the overall UN development agenda, just as I am proud of what was achieved in this sphere during my year as PGA.[10]

Nevertheless, sustainable development remains a complex challenge, encompassing matters such as: How can nations best provide their citizens with effective social safety nets in times of need? How can countries deal with the effects of the global employment crisis? How can member states make economic growth more sustainable, inclusive, and equitable? How can such growth continue without exhausting our natural resources or disrupting the environment?[11]

We need to connect the dots between issues and to make policies that are coherent, effective, and beneficial for all. The High-Level Panel on Global Sustainability is examining the drivers of change that are reshaping our world—issues such as environmental and resource constraints, market volatility, and demographic trends. There are also powerful forces for positive change: expanded democratization, people's empowerment, and gender equality. Indeed, sustainable development is all the more important today in our globalized society.[12]

Supporting sustainable development requires integrated solutions and a global partnership, including South-South and triangular cooperation, as well as broad public participation. There is no doubt that the success of our efforts will require longer-term vision as well as the genuine willingness of member states to ensure that future generations have a better quality of life.[13]

Extreme Poverty and Food Insecurity

It is deeply lamentable that extreme poverty still exists in so many parts of the world, despite the remarkable social and economic development of the past few centuries. The importance that the international community attaches to this issue is symbolized by the election of the eradication of extreme poverty and hunger as the very first of the Millennium Development Goals.

Encouragingly, the world is on track to meet the MDG target of halving the proportion of people living on less than one dollar a day between 1990 and 2015. However, progress is very much concentrated in the significant improvement of living conditions in Asia and, thus, highly imbalanced within the developing world.

The world financial and economic crisis has compounded this imbalance, hitting the most vulnerable countries and social groups the hardest. Even if the global target is achieved by 2015, we cannot forget that many countries will lag behind. And even within the countries that do meet the target, there will be a very large number of individuals still living in poverty.

On October 15, 2011, we commemorated the International Day for the Eradication of Poverty, which was established by the General Assembly in 1993. During the 66th session, the organizers of this ceremony chose the theme "From Poverty to Sustainability: People at the Centre of Inclusive Development." Its formulation was inspired by the lessons of Father Joseph Wresinski, among them that no one should be left aside in the fight against poverty; that extreme poverty is the work of mankind and thus can be ended; that the effective fight against poverty requires empowerment of and ownership by those persons most affected by that scourge; and that actions taken to combat poverty require constant evaluation based on the conditions of those who are worse off. It will be necessary to keep these lessons in mind as we work together toward the full achievement of the MDGs.[14]

Perhaps the most fundamental need associated with extreme poverty is hunger. Today, nearly one billion people are victims of food insecurity and undernourishment on a daily basis. Malnutrition has a particularly lasting impact on children, whose development and growth are stunted. By the year 2050, many of the world's poorest countries and regions will see their populations double. As a result, demand will rapidly expand, and food production will need to markedly increase.

On October 27, 2011, we commemorated the thirty-first observance of World Food Day and the sixty-sixth anniversary of the founding of the Food and Agriculture Organization, a UN specialized agency based in Rome that works to achieve food security for all—to make sure people have regular access to enough high-quality food to lead active, healthy lives.[15] We came together to raise awareness of world hunger and to show our solidarity in the global struggle against hunger, malnutrition, and poverty. We came together to reaffirm the right of all human beings to live in dignity, free from hunger, food insecurity, and malnutrition. And we came together to renew and strengthen commitments made, to forge cooperation, and to enhance political action to address food insecurity.

We need to act today to be prepared for future challenges. Compounding this problem is the need to face climate change and its impacts on people and agriculture. In the short run, targeted safety nets and social programs are essential for alleviating hunger and poverty, while at the same time providing a foundation for development.

Granting market access for agricultural products from developing countries will help in this respect. And small and medium-sized farmers should be supported through increased resource allocation in rural infrastructure and agricultural services. This will be of particular support to agriculture and livelihood recovery efforts, particularly in the Horn of Africa.

Over the longer term, a food-security strategy that relies on a combination of boosting local production and productivity and a general increased role for trade will help to reduce price volatility, while improving food availability and accessibility.[16] But we have also learned, in recent years, that effective regulation and coordinated policy responses are imperative to keep markets running smoothly. Indeed, during the opening of the 66th session of the General Assembly, His Excellency Mr. Leonel Fernandez, president of the Dominican Republic, called on the UN to recognize that commodity derivatives markets have increased the volatility of food and related commodity prices.

On December 27, 2011, I attended a meeting in the historic and beautiful city of Santo Domingo, Dominican Republic, in celebration of the adoption, by consensus, on December 22, of resolution 66/188, "Excessive Price Volatility in Food and Related Financial and Commodity Markets."[17] The following April, we held a high-level thematic debate of the United Nations General Assembly on the topic "Addressing Excessive Price Volatility in Food and Related Commodity Markets." The debate, which gathered an esteemed group of panelists, reflected a deep concern among member states about the impact that excessive commodity price volatility has on food security and sustainable development.

This shared concern was formally expressed in General Assembly resolution 66/188, which was adopted on December 22, 2011. That resolution recognizes "the need to improve the adequate regulation, functioning, and transparency of financial and commodity markets in order to address commodity price volatility." It also "stresses the need to take active measures to reduce excessive food price volatility, while acknowledging that there is an incomplete understanding of its causes and more research needs to be done."[18]

It is understandable that some people in the UN may feel that the issues of financial regulation are best left to technical experts. Yet the role of political deliberation is not to define technical solutions or to replace working institutions but to decide whether and when an issue has arisen with sufficient urgency that new directives must be given and new approaches considered.[19]

Food security depends to a large extent on the availability of clean, safe water. Yet, as populations continue to grow, water shortages remain one of the greatest obstacles to human survival. There are now seven billion people on our planet who each consume between two and four liters of water every day.

The UN system plays an important role by supporting countries in achieving the goals of the Johannesburg Plan of Implementation and the International Decade for Action "Water for Life" (2005–2015). Agreed at the world Summit on Sustainable Development in 2002, the Johannesburg Plan builds on the progress made and lessons learned since the Earth Summit and provides for a more focused approach, with concrete steps and quantifiable and time-bound targets and goals.[20] The International Decade for Action "Water for Life" (2005–2015) seeks to promote efforts to fulfill international commitments made on water and water-related issues by 2015. The Decade started on World Water Day, March 22, 2005. It is intended to focus attention on action-oriented activities and policies that ensure the long-term sustainable management of water resources, in terms of both quantity and quality, and that include measures to improve sanitation. The United Nations is responsible for coordinating the Decade through its interagency coordination mechanism, UN-Water.[21]

Already, almost two billion people have gained access to improved drinking water between 1990 and 2010. The UN also supports member states in meeting emerging challenges. It promotes cooperation at all levels and helps build capacity in integrated water resources management, facilitating access to safe drinking water and the provision of sanitation services.

Despite our concerted efforts to date, much more has to be done to address the needs of the eight hundred million people who still drink dirty water. Forty percent of those still without access to improved drinking water live in Africa. The International Year of Water Cooperation in 2013 should serve as a platform to unify our efforts. Declared by the General Assembly in 2010, the International Year of Water Cooperation will bring together the UN system, governments, civil society, and the business community to increase awareness of water-related problems and to consider ways to resolve them.

Important efforts are being made toward the efficient and sustainable use of limited water resources, the effective application of science and technology, and investment in irrigated agriculture. These efforts should focus as much on economic development and income generation as on food security. Water is life. Without water there can be no future.[22]

Desertification and Land Degradation

Desertification is one of the most complex challenges of our time. It has serious environmental, economic, political, and social effects impacting people, most of whom are poor. According to estimates by the United Nations Environmental Programme, one-quarter of our Earth's land is threatened by desertification, and the livelihoods of over one billion people in more than one hundred countries are jeopardized by desertification. Desertification also threatens to critically undermine gains achieved in sustainable development. The economic, social, and human costs of desertification are tremendous.

Countries in East Africa are experiencing the worst drought in sixty years. In the fall of 2011, this famine claimed the lives of tens of thousands of Somali children under the age of five and caused possibly permanent social disruption as people were forced to move from their communities. This is the most severe food crisis in the world today, and it still requires urgent and concerted action at the global level.

On September 20, 2011, the General Assembly held a high-level meeting with the theme "Addressing Desertification, Land Degradation and Drought in the Context of Sustainable Development and Poverty Eradication." It marked the first time the General Assembly has discussed desertification at the level of heads of state. Over one hundred world leaders participated. Global attention to addressing natural resource scarcity and land degradation has no doubt been on the increase, particularly in connection with the challenges of climate change and food insecurity. However, our common efforts thus far have fallen short.

Effective restoration and rehabilitation of degraded lands and dry lands requires the design of new policies and technologies that promote sustainable resource use as well as predictable financial resources to support domestic initiatives. These strategies must ensure the active engagement of all stakeholders and local communities.

States most affected by desertification have begun to understand the importance of building on their own country-led initiatives and are collaborating to form South-South, triangular, and global alliances that allow them to share technological and policy solutions. These include a proposal made by the State of Qatar in September 2010 for a group of dry-land countries to join together to form the Global Dry Land Alliance. The innovative solutions and best practices developed by the alliance could be shared broadly with dry-land countries throughout the world. Another example is the African Union's Great Green Wall

Initiative, which aims to tackle both environmental and poverty-related challenges by planting a wall of trees across Africa from Senegal in the east to Djibouti in the west.[23]

On October 13, 2011, the Republic of Korea hosted the tenth meeting of the Conference of the Parties to the United Nations Convention to Combat Desertification (COP10). (Generally, two-thirds of the member states must ratify a convention for it to enter into force.)[24] The COP10 meeting was the occasion for my first visit to Asia in my capacity as president of the General Assembly. Pursuant to the mandate of resolution 65/160, I presented the outcome of the General Assembly's September meeting on desertification at the opening session of the high-level segment of the COP.[25]

The General Assembly meeting identified four priority actions for addressing desertification, land degradation, and drought (DLDD). The first is to strengthen the scientific understanding of the problem by establishing an advisory panel focused exclusively on DLDD issues. The panel would provide authoritative and expert advice to enhance effective decision-making on measures to reverse DLDD, to effectively build resilience to drought, and to break the nexus between drought and famine.

The second priority action is to address the accelerating trends in land degradation in all ecosystems, not only in the dry lands. If we wait until other ecosystems are degraded and desertified to act, we risk undermining our ability to ensure sustainable development and to realize the MDGs. In this respect, we need enhanced implementation of the United Nations Convention to Combat Desertification and its ten-year strategic plan as a global policy and monitoring framework.

The third priority action is reversing DLDD through a set of measurable, sustainable development targets. It is also necessary to move toward "zero net land degradation." This is part of our commitment to build a land-degradation-neutral world.

The fourth and final priority action is to improve the financing framework for implementing the international strategy to combat land degradation and poverty. Reversing land degradation is a high-yielding investment. Investing in sustainable land management is far more cost-effective than fixing the consequences of neglect. A number of delegations have noted that investment in sustainable land management should be an integral part of shifting to a green economy.

The international community stands ready to take bold steps to address desertification, land degradation, and drought. It is now up to the member states to ensure that the high-level meeting's recommendations are endorsed and implemented for the benefit of affected populations worldwide.[26] The price of inaction would be measured in food insecurity, poverty, forced migration, climate change, deforestation, loss of biodiversity, political instability, and conflict.[27]

Energy Needs

Access to electricity and modern fuels for cooking and heating are basic necessities in everyday life. Yet billions of people lack access to these energy sources. The result is that—beyond individuals' and communities' significant daily hardship—the international community's efforts toward sustainable development and poverty eradication are stunted. Securing access for all to energy services is indeed crucial for meeting the MDGs.

In addition to being an essential element for sustainable development and poverty eradication, universal access to energy goes hand in hand with fighting climate change. By adopting cleaner fossil-fuel technologies and ensuring access to new and renewable energy, countries can also make important steps in the battle to protect the environment.

In December 2010, pursuant to General Assembly resolution 65/151, the UN declared 2012 the International Year of Sustainable Energy for All. This year-long observance provided much-needed focus for the efforts of the United Nations system toward ensuring energy access for populations worldwide and helped promote the sustainable use of traditional energy resources, cleaner technologies, and newer energy sources.[28]

As part of the International Year, it was incumbent on member states and international organizations to take initiatives designed to create an environment that will foster access to energy and energy-related services and the use of new and renewable energy technologies. They pledged to promote innovation and strengthen employment and investment opportunities in order to keep abreast of the growing need for sustainable energy.

There is no doubt that the global energy market has recently experienced significant shifts, including since the "Arab Awakenings" began in spring 2011. It is no secret that the political instability in some MENA countries has injected significant volatility into the international energy market. A new dynamic has thus emerged in the global market, and it is expected to have a lasting impact on global development.[29]

In January 2012, I took part in the fifth annual World Future Energy Summit held in Abu Dhabi, United Arab Emirates, which is also the headquarters of the International Renewable Energy Agency (IRENA). IRENA is an intergovernmental organization that supports countries in their transition to a sustainable energy future. It serves as a platform for international cooperation, a center of excellence, and a repository of policy, technology, resource, and financial knowledge. IRENA promotes the adoption and sustainable use of all forms of renewable energy, including bioenergy, geothermal, hydropower, ocean, solar, and wind energy, in the pursuit of sustainable development, energy access, energy security, and low-carbon economic growth and prosperity. IRENA encourages governments to adopt policies for renewable energy investments, provides practical tools and policy advice to accelerate renewable energy deployment, and facilitates knowledge sharing and technology transfer. Its membership comprises more than one hundred states and the European Union.[30]

The World Future Energy Summit (WFES) is the world's foremost event dedicated to renewable energies, energy efficiency, and clean technologies. The annual gathering includes a conference, an international exhibition, the Project and Finance Village, the Young Future Energy Leaders program, and a number of corporate meetings and concurrent social events.[31] The 2012 Summit was productive. However, for efforts in the field of sustainable development to be successful, there must be cooperation between all the interested parties, including governments, the academic world, companies, and civil society. Global energy prices must remain stable, and environmentally friendly means of using clean fossil fuels, including natural gas, must be found.[32]

In this regard, I commend the initiative by the secretary-general of the United Nations, Ban Ki-moon, which aims to ensure that, by 2030, all parts of the world will enjoy access to sustainable energy, by achieving the following three interlinked global objectives: first, ensuring universal access to modern energy services; second, doubling the rate of improvement in energy efficiency; third, doubling the share of renewable energy in the global energy mix. To that end, an energy campaign will be launched and a study will be conducted into ways of encouraging the private sector to play a greater role in this field.[33]

Climate Change and Loss of Biodiversity

Recent advances in Earth system science confirm that humanity is facing severe risks—risks that negatively impact human development and our very existence on Earth. During the past century, human activities have resulted in a significant increase of greenhouse-gas concentrations in the atmosphere, the destruction of ecosystems, and the depletion of Earth's biodiversity. Economic growth associated with unsustainable patterns of consumption and production is hindering our quest for harmony, both within and between societies, as well as between humankind and the natural environment.

Unfortunately, over the past decade, the international community has not managed to agree on meaningful action on climate change. We are now, for the first time, acknowledging worldwide that the sustainability of life on Earth is a serious question that will drive fundamental decisions in our societies and the world at large.[34] Important efforts are being made to protect the natural environment from further harm.

It was my privilege to attend the special high-level meeting about the Yasuni-ITT Initiative in Ecuador in September 2011. The Yasuni National Park is two and half million acres of tropical rainforest, rich in biodiversity and home to indigenous peoples. I welcome the Yasuni Initiative as a nontechnical but innovative development solution to addressing climate-change challenges. The meeting offered the opportunity to raise political awareness and galvanize political will and commitments to address the grass-roots and interlinked challenges of biodiversity loss.[35]

A week later, I participated in the celebration of World Habitat Day, commemorated each year on the first Monday of October. It is an occasion to reaffirm our collective responsibility to protect the future of the human habitat. The theme of our observance in 2011 was "Cities and Climate Change."

With more than half of humanity living in urban areas, unsustainable demands are being placed on our resources and the environment. High energy consumption and the emission of greenhouse gases from cities, in particular, are straining our climate. The effects of this pressure are being felt, quite literally, around the world. Consider the increased frequency of heat waves and extreme storms, growing water scarcity, and more frequent and intensive droughts and inland floods.

While coastal cities in developed and developing countries are among the most vulnerable in this respect, it is clear that developing countries are hit the hardest. Climate change impacts their overall development, including their ability to achieve the Millennium Development Goals. And as is so often the case, it is vulnerable groups and women who suffer the most.

At the same time, we have before us an opportunity: an opportunity to build new approaches for relieving pressure on ecosystems and human habitats. Cities are centers of innovation. Contained in their urban sprawl is a rich tapestry of people, industries, knowledge, culture, and infrastructure. Cities are often best placed to provide creative solutions to sustainable development. One important area of attention is mitigation strategies that, when adopted by cities, can reduce greenhouse-gas emissions and help to decrease the magnitude and impact of existing and future changes. Creating more low-carbon cities is a worthwhile goal in this respect.

It is too late for climate change to be prevented altogether. Effective adaptation strategies must be designed and implemented to ensure that cities become more resilient to climate risks. We have seen comprehensive climate-change action plans emerging from a number of major cities, and I call on member states and their partners to consider scaling these up. If we plan for climate change today, it will be less expensive than rebuilding after worse catastrophes in the future.[36]

On April 18, 2012, we commemorated International Mother Earth Day with an interactive dialogue on the theme "Scientific Findings on the Impacts of Human Activities on the Functioning of the Earth System." This apt theme was selected by member states in General Assembly resolution 66/204 and is an implicit recognition of the importance of ensuring harmony with nature through science and multilateral action.[37]

The contribution of science and innovation in achieving sustainable development cannot be underestimated. I firmly believe that the UN system should support a stronger science-based approach to sustainable development. Member states must continue to support the academic sector as it explores and explains these profound issues. It is clear that we have to do more to address the causes and effects of climate change.[38]

One particularly urgent issue is biodiversity loss. Biodiversity is crucial for our continued existence, and we may be on the verge of the sixth mass extinction if we do not take urgent action. In this regard, I commend the two new landmark protocols recently finalized and adopted: the Nagoya Protocol on Access to Genetic Resources and the Fair and Equitable Sharing of Benefits Arising from Their Utilization, and the Nagoya-Kuala Lumpur Supplementary Protocol on Liability and Redress to the Cartagena Protocol on Biosafety.[39]

The Nagoya Protocol on Access to Genetic Resources and the Fair and Equitable Sharing of Benefits Arising from Their Utilization to the Convention on Biological Diversity is an international agreement that aims at sharing the benefits arising from the utilization of genetic resources in a fair and equitable way, including by appropriate access to genetic resources and by appropriate transfer of technologies. It was adopted by the Conference of the Parties to the Convention on Biological Diversity at its tenth meeting in Nagoya, Japan, in 2010.[40]

The Nagoya-Kuala Lumpur Supplementary Protocol on Liability and Redress to the Cartagena Protocol on Biosafety provides international rules and procedure on liability and redress for damage to biodiversity resulting from living modified organisms. It was adopted in 2010 in Nagoya by the governing body of the Cartagena Protocol on Biosafety.[41]

As a human race, we have the resources, the scientific knowledge, and the know-how to save our planet. We must come together to take action in the fight against climate change, taking into account the principle of common but differentiated responsibility.

Other Threats to Development

On June 26, 2012, we held an informal debate of the General Assembly on the theme of "Drugs and Crime as a Threat to Development" in commemoration of the International Day against Drug Abuse and Illicit Trafficking. It also marked the release by the United Nations Office on Drugs and Crime (UNODC) of its World Drug Report 2012, which provides an in-depth review of the tidal movements and flows of illicit drugs across the globe.[42] The report has been very useful in helping us to understand the complete picture regarding the international drug problem.

In the past decade, the growth of drugs and crime has undermined sustainable development and shaken political stability. Peace and security are coming under increasing threat, rocked by drug trafficking and criminal activity. Criminal networks are fueling violence, conflict, and terrorism. No country is immune. Worldwide, we observe drugs and crime eroding the rule of law, human rights, and development. Drugs and crime are destroying the trusted relationship between the people and the state. They are undermining democracy, as well as public confidence in the criminal justice system.

Drugs and organized crime are particularly destructive in weak and fragile countries, where they disrupt and damage progress in development, create gaps in income, and also promote violence. They further jeopardize the important progress being made in achieving the Millennium Development Goals.

Recently, the powerful blow dealt to development because of drugs and crime has captured the attention of the international community. In the 2005 World Summit outcome document, the international community adopted a unified stance on a broad array of issues, from concrete steps toward combating poverty and promoting development to unqualified condemnation of all forms of terrorism, along with the acceptance of collective responsibility to protect civilians against genocide and other crimes against humanity. It also expressed grave concern about the negative effects that illicit trades have on development, peace, security, and human rights.[43] During the 66th session, the General Assembly reiterated this concern and noted the increasing vulnerability of states to such crime. The Assembly recognized that the global drug problem undermines socioeconomic and political stability, as well as sustainable development.

The Assembly has also adopted a number of important international conventions on drug control. The UN Convention Against Illicit Traffic in Narcotic Drugs and Psychotropic Substances, the UN Convention on Transnational Crime and its protocols, and the UN Convention Against Corruption constitute the key framework for a global, strategic response.

Confronting organized crime, drug trafficking, and corruption calls for urgent, joint action. Ending the serious problem of drugs and crime is our shared responsibility. It requires practical, efficient, and comprehensive responses at all levels. The outcome of the June debate included a President's Summary, which was transmitted to the Thirteenth UN Congress on Crime Prevention and Criminal Justice to take place in Doha, Qatar, in 2015.

Development and the fight against crime are long-term processes that require our full and persistent attention. It is only by making this fight against crime a central pillar in the development agenda that we can promote a sustainable and effective response. Let us work together to eliminate this serious problem, so we may ensure that all the world's people can live safe, peaceful, and prosperous lives.[44]

The Role of the UN in Global Economic Governance

The United Nations remains the only truly universal and inclusive multilateral forum. Its legitimacy confers incomparable value to its discussions, negotiated agreements, and operational activities. Yet there has been a noticeable marginalization of the United Nations in key areas of economic governance, as well as a weak accountability for commitments made by member states at UN summits and conferences.

The General Assembly, in its resolution 65/94, recognized the need for an inclusive, transparent, and effective multilateral system to better address urgent global challenges and reaffirmed the central role of the United Nations in efforts to find common solutions.[45] The resolution enjoyed an unusually high number of cosponsors—one hundred in total. Accordingly, the secretary-general submitted an analytical report focusing on "global economic governance and development" (A/66/506), prepared in consultation with member states and relevant organizations of the United Nations system.[46]

A central issue is strengthening coordination, cooperation, coherence, and effective policymaking across the United Nations system. There are proposals that call for new structures, for example, the establishment of a new Global Economic Coordination Council within the

United Nations. Others argue for the strengthening of existing bodies such as the Economic and Social Council. When considering these suggestions, member states should seek the best ways to balance effectiveness with inclusiveness and representativeness.

Related tasks are to enhance the functioning and working methods of United Nations organs and their subsidiary machinery, to improve coordination and efficiency at interagency and operational levels, and to enhance engagement with nonstate actors. It is recommended that the performance of United Nations organs and bodies be periodically reviewed and, when necessary, reformed.

Furthermore, there is a compelling and urgent need to strengthen coordination and improve complementarity of efforts between all major informal groups dealing with the global economic and financial system, the United Nations, and other multilateral organizations. Among these informal groups, the Group of Twenty (G20) is the main forum for international cooperation on the most important issues of the global economic and financial agenda. It brings together finance ministers and central bank governors from nineteen countries—Argentina, Australia, Brazil, Canada, China, France, Germany, India, Indonesia, Italy, Japan, the Republic of Korea, Mexico, Russia, Saudi Arabia, South Africa, Turkey, the United Kingdom, the United States—plus the European Union. The objectives of the G20 are coordinating policy in order to achieve global economic stability and sustainable growth, promoting financial regulations that reduce risks and prevent financial crises, and modernizing the international financial architecture. The G20 was formally established in 1999 when finance ministers and central bank governors of seven major industrial countries (Canada, France, Germany, Italy, Japan, the United Kingdom, and the United States) met in Washington, D.C., in the aftermath of the financial crisis of 1997–1998.[47]

Other key informal groups include the Group of Eight (G8), which comprises Canada, France, Germany, Italy, Japan, the Russian Federation, the United Kingdom, and the United States, as well as the European Union. Members meet annually to deal with the major economic and political issues facing their domestic societies and the inter-national community.[48] Another important group is the Global Gover-nance Group (3G), launched in 2010, which brings together small- and medium-sized countries to develop coordination and cooperation be-tween G20 members and nonmembers, also making the G20 process more consultative, inclusive, and transparent.[49] It currently has thirty members. These informal groups—the G20, the G8, and the 3G—should also strive to collaborate among themselves, since they are ad-dressing issues that are of interest to all.

The recently established practice of convening informal meetings of the General Assembly before and after the G20 Summits, such as I did in October and November 2011, represents an important step toward better coordination between the UN and an important informal group of member states.

Moreover, there is a critical need to ensure greater voice for and par-ticipation of developing countries in the major institutions of global economic governance. This is essential if these institutions are to appro-priately respond to the new challenges of globalization and the reali-ties of the twenty-first century. In this context, it is important to better incorporate regional arrangements into the architecture of global gov-ernance. There is significant scope for strengthening, consolidating, and establishing regional mechanisms, including linkages between regional and global processes. The UN regional commissions are already playing a useful role in this regard.[50]

Governments and the UN cannot tackle development challenges alone. On April 25, 2012, I attended the tenth annual International Forum of the Convention of Independent Financial Advisors (CIFA) in the beautiful Principality of Monaco. CIFA has sought to establish regular dialogue and affiliation with the UN and has been accredited as a nongovernmental organization with special consultative status before the Economic and Social Council. The theme of the event was "What Challenges for the International Financial System? Ethics, Poli-tics, and Finance."

The organization's concerns about how we can achieve more balanced, steady, inclusive, and sustainable development is very much at the heart of the deliberations on economic and development issues in the United Nations General Assembly. Nominal increases in asset prices which are not sustainable cannot contribute materially to economic growth.

The UN International Conference on Financing for Development in Monterrey in 2002, and the resulting "Monterrey Consensus," initiated the practice of yearly meetings between ECOSOC and the Bretton Woods institutions plus the World Trade Organization and the Secretariat of the United Nations Conference on Trade and Development (UNCTAD).

These yearly meetings take place a few weeks before the important spring ministerial meetings of the Bretton Woods institutions so that ECOSOC might have the opportunity to provide input into the spring meetings. In 2008, two major events took place. The first was the followup to the Monterrey conference that was held in Doha. The second was the beginning of the world financial and economic crisis.

After difficult negotiations in Doha—negotiations that touched on the need to significantly overhaul the Bretton Woods institutions and their relation to the UN—a compromise was reached. Member states called for a General Assembly high-level conference on the world financial and economic crisis and its impact on development, which was held in June 2009.

Member states' positions at this conference were driven by their diverse political interests and concerns. During the 66th session, issues surrounding the institutional response to the crisis remained very contentious among the membership of the UN. Nonetheless, the secretary-general issued a report on global economic governance, and the Assembly adopted two resolutions on the topic. The second of these, which was adopted during my presidency, reiterated the need for inclusive, transparent, and effective multilateral approaches to managing global challenges and in this regard reaffirmed the central role of the United Nations in its ongoing efforts to find common solutions to such challenges.[51]

On May 17 and 18, 2012, we held a high-level debate on the theme "State of the World Economy and Finance in 2012" at UN Headquarters, which I cochaired with the secretary-general, His Excellency Mr. Ban Ki-moon. The global economy was at a critical juncture, facing pressing economic and financial issues that needed to be tackled to achieve a robust, sustained, and inclusive global recovery—a recovery that will accelerate development, improve employment, and lift another billion people out of poverty.

This conference was the first of its kind. In preparation, I went to Washington, D.C., and met with the IMF and World Bank, which welcomed the idea, as did the World Trade Organization and the European Union. To make the event as successful as possible, the secretary-general and I sent an invitation signed by both of us inviting all heads of state and government along with their foreign ministers and ministers of finance. Of course, I also invited the private sector including high-level executives of major banks.

We spent two days discussing the current global economic crisis and its impact on both developed and developing countries. Developing countries, in particular, have been affected by circumstances that were not of their own making. Moreover, within all countries, it has been the vulnerable sections of society—the poor—who have been hardest hit by the downturn in incomes and in employment.

Today, in the great spirit of democracy, populations are making their concerns about the global economy heard. They are demanding more economic safety, more jobs, more opportunities, more justice, and more respect for the environment. Member states have varied in their responses to these demands. In a diverse world, this is only natural. However, the UN's priority must be to implement an effective and globally coordinated policy that serves to place the world economy on the path of sustained growth and development.

Over the past twenty years, there has been significant progress in the development of a rules-based international trading system but very little movement toward a rules-based international monetary and financial system. Important, unfinished tasks include enhancing multilateral oversight, improving oversight of the world's important financial institutions, strengthening the transparency of risk-rating mechanisms, and improving regional financial cooperation. It is also important to broaden and strengthen the participation of developing countries in international economic decision-making and norm-setting.[52]

Without doubt, the high-level debate served to advance the dialogue on the policies necessary to stimulate the global economy and advance economic development across the world. The high-level representation and diversity of participants at this meeting, as well as the rich array of viewpoints that were shared, are clear indications of the inclusive nature and unique convening power of the United Nations. I would like to highlight some key messages that emerged from the round-table discussions.

Roundtable 1 focused on "combating unemployment, creating jobs, especially for women and youth, addressing poverty and social protection." Unemployment, especially youth unemployment, remains exceptionally high, particularly in countries facing sovereign-debt problems. Meanwhile, many workers in developing countries continue to face unemployment challenges, poor pay, vulnerable job conditions, and lack of access to any form of social security. In that context, we need policy packages that realize decent work and promote nationally designed social protection floors, as called for in UN and other specialized agencies' reports.

Roundtable 2 covered the issues pertaining to "debt sustainability, managing inflation and deflation." The world financial and economic crisis caused a sharp increase of the debt ratios in many countries. While there is a need for credible fiscal consolidation and government debt reduction in the long run, countries should avoid excessive austerity measures that may hinder economic recovery. Moreover, we need to continue to improve multilateral frameworks to assess debt sustainability and improve early warning signals of debt distress. Independent debt workout mechanisms may help prevent future crises as well.

Roundtable 3 focused on "creating an environment for increasing production, trade, and investment, including through transparency and predictability of commodity prices." It is necessary that governments create an enabling business environment that encourages both domestic and foreign investment. Technical assistance by donors can play an important role in that regard.

It is also important to avoid trade protectionism and to reach a successful conclusion of the Doha round of trade negotiations with a balanced, ambitious, comprehensive, and development-oriented outcome. Moreover, there is a need to urgently address the root causes and problems created by excessive commodity price volatility, including through greater economic diversification and the promotion of transparency and market information at all levels.

Roundtable 4 addressed the issue of "increasing stability, predictability, and transparency in the global financial system." The international community has undertaken important efforts to draw the right lessons from the financial crisis. Nonetheless, we need to continue our work to make the financial sector safer and more stable and to put it back on the path of serving the real economy and our shared development goals. In this ongoing process of reforming and strengthening the international financial system, it is crucial that the concerns of developing countries are duly taken into account.[53]

Our recommendations for avoiding future financial crises are collected in a "Chair's Summary," which I transmitted to all member states.[54] The major lesson from the global financial and economic crisis is simple: the existing structures of global economic governance have not adequately evolved to reflect the interconnected economic and geopolitical realities of today's world. Recent years have witnessed a rising desire and demand for the rebalancing of global economic power, especially as we see the increased economic importance of emerging market economies. We must act collectively to find solutions to problems regarding, for example, multilateral trade, migration, sovereign debt, and tax cooperation.

With the cooperation of the private sector, the UN and its various bodies are well equipped to advance the health of our global economy, so it might nourish every person in every village, in every town, every city, and every nation across the world.[55] For over sixty years, ECOSOC has served as an important forum where member states could assemble to collectively address global development challenges. The strength of ECOSOC and its subsidiary bodies has always lain in its broad representation and in its opportunity for countries large and small to voice their concerns and seek solutions to common global problems. I commend the members of the council and its bureau for their efforts to make ECOSOC and its subsidiary bodies even more effective.

Every year, ECOSOC holds its ministerial review to assess progress toward achieving the internationally agreed development goals. In the aftermath of the global financial and economic crisis and the resulting jobs crisis, the 2012 session appropriately focused on productive capacity, employment, and decent work.

Unemployment, particularly of women, youth, and disadvantaged groups, is one of the world's biggest challenges. The International Labour Organization estimated a further increase in global unemployment to two hundred million in 2012. Of this number, seventy-five million are young people and eighty-four million are women. Inclusive, sustainable, and equitable economic growth—as well as full employment—is crucial to poverty eradication, achieving the MDGs, and maximizing long-term gains in real incomes.[56]

In April 2012, I traveled to Doha, in my home country of Qatar, to participate in the thirteenth high-level session of the United Nations Conference on Trade and Development (UNCTAD13). Following the previous session in the Ghanaian capital, Accra, in 2008, the world had witnessed substantial challenges in international trade and development, particularly the global economic crisis. Therefore, the main theme chosen for this session, "Development-Centred Globalization: Towards

Inclusive and Sustainable Growth and Development," was most timely and appropriate.

UNCTAD was established in 1964 to fill a void in the institutional framework created during the climactic years of World War Two, to manage international economic affairs. It was intended to complement two important United Nations conferences that took place in the 1940s. The first was held at Bretton Woods in 1944 and established two of the main pillars of the postwar international architecture: the World Bank and the International Monetary Fund. The second was the United Nations Conference on Trade and Employment that gave rise to the General Agreement on Tariffs and Trade (GATT) in 1946.

The main purpose of those institutions, understandably, was to avoid a repetition of the Great Depression and of the world war that it helped ignite. As such, the Bretton Woods institutions were focused primarily on establishing rules and mechanisms for harmonizing policies and coordinating policy action among the leading economic powers of the day. Their role in fostering economic development was clearly secondary.

Twenty years later, UNCTAD was organized by the General Assembly of the United Nations Organization to deal with a fundamental new reality: the wave of decolonization that swept across the world, forever changing the constituency of the still very young United Nations. UNCTAD was the expression of this new geopolitical map, of the high hopes the world entertained for facilitating the entry of the large number of newly independent and rising nations into world commerce and trade. This history indeed binds UNCTAD to the General Assembly in a way that is unique among the UN structures.

UNCTAD's special vocation has been, from the start, to take a comprehensive view of the constantly evolving challenges facing developing countries. Its agenda has, from its inception, prominently included issues of money and finance, as well as aid and access to technology. It has also included what was once referred to as "institutional arrangements, methods, and machinery," which we today call "systemic reform" and "global governance."

Where I think UNCTAD has been most successful has been in helping member states to think creatively and constructively about promoting developmental change; foreseeing change and its consequences; and providing essential tools to strengthen member states' capacities to foster, and at times cope with, economic change. It has also been most effective when it has helped to direct ideas and resources to provide clear and usable policy guidance.

Underlying all my initiatives, efforts, and words on matters of development is my firm belief that the United Nations and its General Assembly must play a more prominent role in global economic governance. There must be greater accountability for commitments made by member states at UN summits and conferences.[57]

Financing for Development

On December 7, 2011, we held the fifth High-Level Dialogue on Financing for Development. Following two years of a fragile and uneven recovery, there was widespread concern over another major global economic downturn. Threats included the sovereign-debt crises in Europe, the continuing jobs crisis in developed countries, weaknesses in the financial sector, and volatile food and energy prices. Moreover, political divides over how to tackle these problems and calls for fiscal austerity were impeding effective and coordinated policy responses.

Strong and sustained global economic recovery is necessary for developing countries to effectively mobilize domestic resources for development. Fragilities in the global economy—including the risk of spillovers from developed countries, reversals in private capital inflows, exchange-rate misalignments, and commodity price volatility—continue to hamper their growth prospects.

Given this environment, it is critical that developing countries undertake measures to address poverty and to expand productive employment opportunities. To finance such measures on a sustained basis, considerable levels of external assistance are required. Short-term portfolio equity flows to developing countries went into a tailspin in the second half of 2011, in line with the high volatility that is typical for these flows. Given their volatile nature, greater consideration should be given to measures that mitigate their potential destabilizing effect.

Foreign direct investment (FDI) flows to developing countries are likely to be adversely affected in the event of a renewed slowdown in the global economy, too. This is worrisome, as FDI tends to be more stable and long-term in nature compared to other private flows.

The development potential of international trade continues to be limited by a wide range of tariff and nontariff restrictions as well as agricultural subsidies in developed countries. Consequently, it remains imperative to arrive at a successful and development-oriented conclusion to the Doha round of multilateral trade negotiations.

At the Cannes Summit, G-20 leaders reiterated their support for the Doha Development Agenda mandate and stressed the need for fresh, credible approaches to furthering trade negotiations, including issues of concern for the least developed countries (LDCs). The LDCs represent the poorest and weakest segment of the international community. They comprise more than 880 million people (about 12 percent of the world population) but account for less than 2 percent of world gross domestic product (GDP) and about 1 percent of global trade in goods. The General Assembly established this category in 1971 to attract international support.[58]

The Economic and Social Council uses three criteria for identifying LDCs: a low-income criterion, based on a three-year-average estimate of the gross national income (GNI) per capita (under $750 for inclusion, above $900 for graduation); a human resource weakness criterion, involving an index based on indicators of nutrition, health, education, and adult literacy; and an economic vulnerability criterion, involving an index based on indicators of instability of agricultural production and exports, the share of manufacturing and services in the economy, merchandise export concentration, and the handicap of economic smallness. To be added to the list, a country must satisfy all three criteria.[59]

The current list includes forty-nine countries: Afghanistan, Angola, Bangladesh, Benin, Bhutan, Burkina Faso, Burundi, Cambodia, Central African Republic, Chad, Comoros, Democratic Republic of the Congo, Djibouti, Equatorial Guinea, Eritrea, Ethiopia, the Gambia, Guinea, Guinea-Bissau, Haiti, Kiribati, the Lao People's Democratic Republic, Lesotho, Liberia, Madagascar, Malawi, Mali, Mauritania, Mozambique, Myanmar, Nepal, Niger, Rwanda, Samoa, Sao Tome and Principe, Senegal, Sierra Leone, Solomon Islands, Somalia, South Sudan, the Sudan, Tanzania, Timor-Leste, Togo, Tuvalu, Uganda, Vanuatu, Yemen, and Zambia.[60]

After almost a decade of multilateral trade negotiations, the share of LDCs in world trade remains extremely low. It is important for the international community to deliver on our promise to provide duty-free and quota-free access for all products originating from LDCs and to increase resources for Aid for Trade to enable poorer countries to enhance their trade competitiveness.

Given the continuing economic difficulties faced by developing countries in the aftermath of the global financial crisis, it is imperative that developed countries fulfill all their commitments regarding official development assistance (ODA). In 2010, ODA reached a record level of US$128.7 billion—or 0.32 percent of OECD/DAC members' combined gross national income. However, many larger donors remain below the United Nations target of 0.7%.

There continues to be an urgent need to increase the volume, quality, and reliability of aid flows to meet the internationally agreed development goals, including the MDGs. I would also like to emphasize here the potential of innovative financing mechanisms to complement existing ODA.

Despite improved external debt indicators in a number of developing countries, there remain concerns about debt sustainability, which could be adversely affected by spillover effects from the European debt crisis and other risk factors, such as volatile energy and food prices and exchange-rate instability. The effectiveness of debt-sustainability frameworks need to be reexamined through further work at the inter-agency level. Efforts are also needed to design instruments and institutional mechanisms to better deal with debt distress.[61]

In June 2012, we held a retreat in Tarrytown, New York, on UN operational activities for development. The retreat was the culmination of a three-part seminar series leading up to the 2012 General Assembly quadrennial comprehensive policy review (QCPR) of operational activities for development of the UN system. Through the quadrennial comprehensive policy review of operational activities for development of the United Nations system, the General Assembly defines the way the United Nations development system operates to support countries in their development efforts. The review deals with funding of United Nations operational activities for development, the functioning of the United Nations development system, and the effectiveness of the work of the United Nations system for development.

The issue of funding is vital for the effectiveness of UN operational activities for development. Core resources are generally seen as a more efficient way of building relevant and effective partnerships with program countries in the delivery of operational activities for development. Core resources provide the highest quality and flexibility of pooled funding. They are critical for ensuring the entities' capacity to deliver on their multilateral mandates. They are also needed to provide continued substantive leadership and innovation around specific goals, advocacy, and policy work, in addition to programmatic implementation on the ground. Furthermore, core resources are central to ensuring the entities' independence, neutrality, and role as trusted partners in a changing development cooperation landscape.

While long-term trends in funding to the UN development system have been favorable, the core/noncore imbalance continues to grow. It is enigmatic that, while noncore resources to cover the activities of the organization have increased, the mandates depending on the core resources remain underfunded.

The practical implications of this declining share of core resources are evident at the country level. For example, at the outset of many new United Nations Development Assistance Framework (UNDAF) projects, assured funding through core resources can be as low as 30 percent of planned programming by the UN development system. The UNDAF is a strategic program document between a government and the United Nations organizations in the country (the country team) describing the actions and strategies of the UN system for national development. The UNDAF defines outcomes, activities, and United Nations agency responsibilities.[62] If the share of core resources allocated to this system declines further, there is a real risk that it will lose its ability to mobilize noncore funding for country-level programming.

The resident coordinator system is at the core of UN coherence at the country level. It seeks to bring together the different United Nations agencies in a country to improve the efficiency and effectiveness of operational activities. It encompasses all organizations of the United Nations system dealing with operational activities for development. Resident coordinators, who are funded and managed by the UNDP, lead United Nations country teams in more than 130 countries, work closely with the government, and are the representatives of the secretary-general for development operations.[63] However, the resident coordinator is not the resident manager of the UN development system in program countries. Thus, he or she has to rely to a large extent on his or her personal attributes and leadership skills to enlist support from the UN country team.

It is interesting in this context to go back in time and see that this was not the original vision in General Assembly resolution 32/197, adopted in 1977 for country-level coordination of the UN development system. In this resolution, the Assembly endorsed the concept of a single UN officer being responsible for coordinating all UN operational activities at the country level.[64]

The survey of program countries that was conducted in preparation for the report of the secretary-general for the 2012 QCPR has revealed that governments feel it is very important to strengthen the coordination role of the UN resident coordinator. In my view, a new General Assembly resolution is needed to address this issue.

Promoting greater coherence among the development, humanitarian, peacekeeping, and political pillars of the United Nations work in many transition countries is critical to the success of the organization's work in those challenging situations. The concept of integration, introduced by the secretary-general in 2008, has begun to make a difference in enhancing the effectiveness of the United Nations system in those countries or areas that have adopted the integrated mission concept.

Looking forward, the UN development system, in order to remain relevant and effective, will increasingly have to tailor its support to different country contexts. Middle-income countries, with stronger state capacities and greater access to resources, increasingly challenge the effectiveness of the traditional approach to development cooperation. Between 2005 and 2011, some eighteen low-income countries moved to the middle-income status.

The QCPR process has revealed many innovations in the functioning of the UN development system in middle-income countries. In that context, I would highlight the introduction by UN country teams of lighter instruments for program planning and implementation. For example, in Cape Verde, a joint office model has been developed.[65]

In middle-income countries, where governments have implementation capacity and access to resources, we must find the right balance between traditional development assistance and upstream support. In turn, the country presence and funding system of UN entities should also be adapted to this evolving business model in middle-income countries.[66]

South-South Cooperation

South-South cooperation is based on a philosophy of solidarity—solidarity that unites developing countries through partnerships and alliances, so that they may gain an effective voice in the international arena as they negotiate and advance their shared interests.

South-South relations are gaining significant importance on the development landscape. In recent decades, both the potential and the prospects of the global South have improved markedly. This rise is reflected in increased resources, life expectancy, school attendance, and other indicators of human well-being. The emergence of the South has led to a significant shift in the geopolitical balance. However, the full realization of this potential requires good governance and more South-South cooperation.

There are now stronger South-South ties in the form of regional and subregional organizations, such as the African Union, the South American Community of Nations, the Gulf Cooperation Council, and ASEAN, to name but a few. These regional arrangements also provide useful forums for development activities and should be further enhanced. Such cooperation can be challenging yet remains essential.

One of the particular strengths of South-South cooperation is its framework for countries to pool their human, financial, and other resources to meet shared development needs. We have been pleased to witness the numerous jobs created owing to growing flows of South-South trade, investment, remittances, and development assistance.

I had the honor of presiding over the High-level Committee on South-South Cooperation between 2007 and 2009 and am proud to have concluded my term of office with the successful adoption of the Nairobi outcome document in December 2009.[67] I am pleased to know that the Special Unit has, on behalf of the secretary-general, prepared the framework of operational guidelines for use by United Nations entities and agencies in implementing the Nairobi outcome document.

I have also had the privilege to personally witness the establishment of the SS-GATE and attended three of the Annual Global South-South Development Expos, which the Special Unit organized with the support and participation of more than twenty UN entities.[68]

In December 2011, I attended the 2011 Global South-South Development Expo in Rome. The experience strengthened my conviction that South-South and triangular cooperation, backed by adequate funding, are key tools for tackling the development challenges of our time. Among such challenges, guaranteeing food security for all is paramount, and I commend 2011's South-South Expo for focusing on food security.

The South-South Expo offered an opportunity to examine holistic approaches to food security. We exchanged lessons learned and showcased successful Southern strategies and technologies for, among other things, improving agricultural productivity, increasing social protection and building the resilience of the most vulnerable, managing fragile ecosystems, improving nutrition, and combating diseases.

We also looked at renewable energy sources and agribusiness models that are working to put sufficient nutritious food on the table. Many Southern countries have lifted millions of people out of conditions of extreme poverty and hunger. Their knowledge and technical know-how can be put to further good use through enhanced South-South exchanges of information, experience, and technology, with a view to raising agricultural productivity and to improving food distribution to the benefit of more populations.

Initiatives such as the Global Dry Land Alliance and the African Union's Great Green Wall, mentioned earlier, are designed to support and complement efforts toward tangible progress in achieving the MDGs, particularly MDG 1, "Eradicate Extreme Poverty and Hunger," and MDG 7, "Ensure Environmental Sustainability." Through South-South solidarity, we can also learn from countries that are reforming customary norms and practices in order to ensure that women are no longer denied equal access to land and other productive assets that contribute to food security. In doing so, women will be empowered and can gain their rightful place in society.

Investment in agricultural research is another important area for South-South cooperation. It can help improve funding for research on tropical crops, on which millions of poor people in the South depend.

Partnerships that engage leading agricultural institutions in the global South would go a long way to strengthen the capacity of all Southern countries to feed their citizens, to raise production capacities, and to gainfully participate in food supply chains created to meet rising food demands in rapidly growing populations.

As PGA and since, I have remained committed to promoting South-South and triangular cooperation as an important part of building a united global partnership. I applaud those Southern countries—from Asia to Africa to Latin America—that are already actively involved in these types of exchanges, and I am thankful to those Northern countries that support triangular cooperation. It is my hope that these exchanges, programs, and partnerships will be replicated and adapted widely.[69]

The Least Developed Countries

On September 26, 2011, I attended the annual ministerial meeting of the least developed countries (LDCs), forty-eight countries classified by the United Nations as "least developed." The LDCs continue to be among the most vulnerable nations of the world. Global attention on the major challenges they face is often lacking, unless they are engulfed in conflict or devastated by natural disasters. We saw this in recent years with the tsunami in the Maldives, the earthquake in Haiti, and the drought in Somalia.

The current global financial crisis, as well as the worldwide rise in food and fuel prices, has accentuated vulnerability in the LDCs. As a result, important domestic programs aimed at reducing poverty, promoting sustainable development, and meeting the basic needs are at risk. As PGA, I sought to accord the most vulnerable countries, most of whom are LDCs, the much-needed support they deserve.

An important issue before us during the 66th session was how to best follow up on the Istanbul Declaration and Programme of Action (IPOA), which was agreed by member states in May 2011.[70] The Istanbul Programme of Action contains important steps for eradicating poverty, achieving internationally agreed development goals, and reaching the objective of the graduation of half of all LDCs by 2020.[71]

In December 2011, the General Assembly adopted resolution 66/213, recommended in the report of the Second Committee on the implementation of the Fourth United Nations Conference on the Least Developed Countries. Operative paragraph 16 of that resolution "requests the President of the General Assembly to establish, in consultation with member states and the Secretary-General, an Ad Hoc Working Group to further study and strengthen the smooth transition process for the countries graduating from the least developed country category and to submit a report to the General Assembly at its sixty-seventh session with specific recommendations, consistent with the Istanbul Programme of Action."[72]

To follow up on this mandate, I undertook extensive consultations with member states, in particular with the major groups that are involved closely in this matter, namely, the LDCs Group, the Group of 77 and China, the European Union, and the Friends of the LDCs, which represent a variety of member states including key development partners as well as with the secretary-general.[73] (The Group of 77, named for the seventy-seven countries that signed the Joint Declaration after the first session of UNCTAD, is now the largest caucus group in the Assembly with over 130 members.)[74]

Under my vigilant guidance, the Ad Hoc Working Group, cofacilitated by Ambassador Jan Grauls of Belgium and Ambassador Brian Bowler of Malawi, convened at UN Headquarters from January 16 to June 6, 2012, and successfully completed its work. The group issued a report (A/67/92) with specific recommendations, consistent with IPOA, including with regard to the graduation of LDCs and the needed smooth transition process for those graduating.[75]

The report emphasizes the need to strengthen the smooth transition process, saying that this can be achieved with better information and understanding of existing support measures and if strong national transition strategies are put in place. It also recommends discussion of transition measures to help build coherence. Additionally, the report underlines the need for continued official development assistance and technical assistance, as well as the need to adapt trade-related measures to changing development situations.

It is also worth noting that the Working Group is open-ended, and any member state that wants to contribute substantively to its work is able to do so. Relevant nonstate-partners, including think tanks, research bodies, development institutions, and private-sector and civil society representatives could also be invited by the cochairs in consultation with the Working Group members. In view of the substantial overlap in the composition of the Group of Small Island Developing States (SIDS) and the Group of Landlocked Developing Countries (LLDCs) with the list of LDCs, I recommended that the chairs of SIDS and LLDCs regularly participate in the activities of the Working Group.[76]

Small island developing states were categorized as a distinct group of developing countries facing specific social, economic, and environmental problems at the 1992 Earth Summit. The United Nations recognizes the thirty-eight United Nations member states belonging to the Alliance of Small Island States, an ad hoc negotiating body established by SIDS at the United Nations. The Alliance also includes fourteen other islands that are not members of the United Nations.[77] At the same time, lack of territorial access to the sea, remoteness and isolation from world markets, and high transit costs continue to impose serious constraints on the socioeconomic development of landlocked developing countries. Of thirty LLDCs, sixteen are classified as least developed.[78] In 2001, the General Assembly adopted resolution 56/227, establishing a high representative for the least developed countries, landlocked developing countries, and small island developing states to advance the cause of those states.[79]

Grave matters of concern facing the LDCs are multifaceted, including the consequences of climate change. We should bear in mind that many of these nations are primarily dependent on agriculture, suffer from lack of sufficient water, or are affected by land degradation and deforestation. Half a dozen Pacific and Indian Ocean small island LDCs, as well as heavily populated countries, such as Bangladesh, are threatened by rising sea levels.

The combined population of LDCs is expected to nearly double between now and 2050, rising from 880 million to 1.8 billion. The combination of extreme poverty, population pressure, and environmental degradation is a powerful destabilizing force for these countries.[80] Common efforts are the only way to tackle the global challenges that disproportionately impact LDCs. We must use the tools at our disposal that privilege inclusion, collaboration, and consensus building. This will ensure that LDCs are heard and their needs are taken into account.[81]

Development in Africa

On October 7, 2011, we held a high-level panel discussion to commemorate the tenth anniversary of the New Partnership for Africa's Development (NEPAD). NEPAD is an African-owned, African-led flagship program for socioeconomic and political development on the continent.

NEPAD's priorities—poverty eradication, sustainable growth, and empowerment of women—echo those of the Millennium Declaration. NEPAD is also the embodiment of African leadership and ownership of its development agenda. For this reason, these two frameworks should guide our joint efforts for Africa's development.

NEPAD has contributed meaningfully to the remarkable economic success and social progress in Africa over the past decade. Social indicators, such as those for education and health, have significantly improved. Recently, Africa has been the home of six out of the ten fastest growing economies in the world. Africa is a growth pole and is increasingly attracting foreign direct investment.

This good performance was underpinned by sound macroeconomic policies and structural reforms, which took place in the context of a more stable political environment that has characterized an increasing number of African countries. The role of the private sector in economies has also expanded. And the African Peer Review Mechanism has improved good governance and rule of law, creating the preconditions for sustainable and broad-based economic growth.

Despite this progress, critical challenges remain. The majority of African countries are unlikely to achieve most of the Millennium Development Goals by the 2015 deadline. It is imperative, therefore, that we redouble our efforts. Focus is needed, in particular, on reducing extreme poverty, creating decent employment, and improving maternal and child health. NEPAD is an essential framework in this respect.

To improve effectiveness and efficiency of partnerships for Africa, and building on the Political Declaration of the Special Needs of Africa in 2008, the General Assembly established a monitoring mechanism to review commitments toward Africa's development needs, building on existing monitoring mechanisms.[82]

While strengthening partnership with NEPAD, it is also important to look beyond aid. We must emphasize the need for a productive global partnership, which includes mutually beneficial trade and investment relationships, as well as the protection of the global climate.[83] On November 22, 2011, we celebrated African Industrialization Day, an annual event for member states to reaffirm their ongoing commitment to mobilizing the international community for the industrialization of Africa. In 2011, we paid special attention to the theme "Sustainable Energy for Accelerated Industrial Development in Africa," underscoring once again that energy infrastructure is a key driver for economic growth. NEPAD's energy program has made tireless efforts to improve energy generation and access across the continent.

Despite this progress, critical challenges remain. Overcoming energy poverty is one such challenge. The sustainable use of traditional energy resources as well as access to efficient, affordable modern energy sources and services are required for African countries to tap into global production networks and to reap the benefits of economies of scale. Job creation, income generation, poverty reduction, and improved quality of life will be the ultimate benefits of sustainable energy.[84]

Rio+20 and Beyond

On June 20, 2012, I had the privilege to address the opening ceremony of the United Nations Conference on Sustainable Development in Rio de Janeiro, Brazil (Rio+20). The government of Brazil spared no effort to ensure the success of this historic event, while showcasing how a developing country can at the same time successfully pursue material prosperity, social fairness, and environmental well-being.

The summit was the opportunity of a generation—a chance to transform ideas and aspirations into bold actions and everyday realities, to shape the future for generations to come. We must strive for a future in which equity, equality, and prosperity are the norm, not the exception. Such a future is possible.

We have testimony that certain policies allow countries to grow and improve living conditions, while protecting the environment. Major advances in science and technology have opened up other new possibilities for sustainable development. We have a lot to learn from each other on what has worked.

We must not let the world financial and economic crisis dampen the commitment to development cooperation. International development cooperation must continue to play a key role in promoting solutions for our global challenges. Development cooperation must become wider and deeper. It must go far beyond development assistance.

Sustainable development is becoming truly a collective endeavor. And it increasingly encompasses many other actors, besides our governments. Twenty years ago, the first Rio conference marked the entry of civil society to the United Nations. It spurred an alliance with NGOs, businesses and industries, farmers, women, and other major groups. Such partnerships are now at the core of efforts to support sustainable development in all countries. It is particularly heartening that young people, yearning for freedom and justice, have become so involved.

The Rio+20 outcome document charts a path for sustainable development for the next twenty years. It defines sustainable development goals, setting the stage as we reflect on the UN development agenda after 2015, the target date for the Millennium Development Goals.[85]

In 1992, Rio was the birthplace of not only Agenda 21 but the three Rio conventions: on climate change, biodiversity, and desertification. I would urge member states to realize their important commitments made in the Agenda and these conventions.

The beautiful city of Rio de Janeiro is the very symbol of efforts made, and of the progress achieved, by Brazilian society in recent years. There could hardly have been a more suitable setting for this conference. The Brazilian composer Antônio Carlos Jobim sings in one of his masterpieces that the waters of March mark the end of the summer, but they are a promise of life to our hearts.[86]

Like the waters of March, Rio+20 was not an end but a new beginning, a promise of a better life for us, for our children, and for future generations.[87] International consensus emerged and agreement was reached in important areas of sustainable development. In the outcome document, titled "The Future We Want," member states renewed their commitments and recognized the importance of their shared responsibility. The real work is in the implementation of this agreement, and we all have our parts to play in its ultimate success.[88]

Sources of Hope

In closing this chapter, I would like to call attention to several events and initiatives that pointed to other valuable sources of hope for sustainable development.

On November 8, 2011, I held an informal briefing on the secretary-general's Global Pulse initiative, which aims to use the tools of science and technology to achieve sustainable development. The UN is uniquely positioned to take advantage of innovations in water management and sanitation, energy, and public health to better protect the poor and those living in the most vulnerable situations.[89]

That same day, we commemorated the twenty-fifth anniversary of the

United Nations Declaration on the Right to Development. The meeting aimed at enhancing policy coherence in the global partnership for development, in line with the statements issued by the Committee on Economic Social Civil Rights, the nine human rights treaty bodies, the seventeen United Nations system agencies, and other international organizations. We gathered to emphasize the importance of the work being conducted and to commit to realizing policy coherence.[90]

On December 2, 2011, we held a forum on the diaspora economy. Diasporas are at the forefront of economic globalization. In recent years, there has been a rise in international awareness of diasporas' important economic contributions, to both their countries of origin and of destination. Our collective action must be directed toward supporting diasporas, so that their contributions to development might achieve their full potential.[91]

In April 2012, I attended the High-Level Meeting on Well-Being and Happiness: Defining a New Economic Paradigm. As member states reaffirmed in resolution 65/309, happiness is a fundamental human goal.[92] As the theme of the meeting suggests, a new economic paradigm is needed: a paradigm that takes into consideration economic growth and environmental protection and tangibly leads to greater well-being and happiness.

The host of the high-level meeting, the royal government of the Kingdom of Bhutan, has developed a unique Bhutanese model for measuring happiness. "Gross national happiness" aims to achieve harmony between the economy, the environment, and spiritual and cultural values. It is considered far more important than gross national product, as it strives for more than material progress and the accumulation of wealth alone. Sustainable development is precisely about balancing economic, environmental, social, and spiritual values. This perfect harmony is what I personally consider to bring happiness, well-being, and prosperity.[93]

On March 7, 2012, we marked International Women's Day: a day when we each recognize and appreciate the fundamental role of women. Yet we are all aware that women do not enjoy the equality they deserve.

Advancing the status of women worldwide is a responsibility we share. This responsibility, and our determination to fulfill it, has been present since the UN's founding days. The UN Charter affirms faith in fundamental human rights, in the dignity and worth of every human person, and in the equal rights of men and women.

This International Women's Day, we paid particular attention to empowering rural women to end hunger and poverty. Women are agents of development. Rural women, in particular, play a critical role in advancing agricultural and rural development, improving food security, and eradicating poverty. They are integral to achieving the Millennium Development Goals and sustainable development as a whole.

We need to do more to empower rural women, so they can reach their full potential as key contributors to the global economy. They need better access to land rights, modern technologies, and financing. They need greater business opportunities. And they need to be protected from all forms of discrimination, inequality, violence, and social exclusion. Special focus in this context needs to be given to girls as well.

We also need to carry out extensive education and awareness-raising campaigns on the rights of women. To empower rural women, more action is needed to improve the active participation of women in all political and economic decision-making processes at the local level. I call on member states, the UN system, and our partners to strengthen their efforts to empower rural women, recognizing their major contribution—both real and potential—to ending hunger and poverty worldwide.[94]

6

Challenges to Human Security

Security as a Framework

While the four pillars elaborated in the previous chapters were the focus of my work as president of the General Assembly, we also sought during the 66th session to address other important challenges such as protection of human rights, disease prevention and control, combating organized crime, and nuclear safety. These concerns for human security are not new. They impact the well-being, livelihood, and dignity of peoples around the world.

People's aspirations are routinely frustrated and left unrealized when they are faced with sudden economic and financial crises, natural disasters, and violent conflicts, as well as with adversities such as human trafficking, outbreaks of disease, and massive displacements. These threats can also evolve into broader and more intractable crises that all too often move from the national and regional levels to become international security challenges.

These are the very issues that we have at the top of our agenda in the General Assembly. As I have noted in previous chapters, the multidimensional nature of contemporary challenges requires more holistic, integrated, and sustainable solutions. The greatest threats facing the world today cannot be solved in isolation. It is in this context that the United Nations can serve in addressing the broader issues surrounding human security.

There is an urgent need to bring policies and institutions together in a far more effective way than the stand-alone or fragmented responses that we have seen in the past. Addressing human security requires that we bring international actors, including entities within the United Nations, together to advance comprehensive and integrated solutions that are focused on people, their protection, and their empowerment.

Human security provides a viable framework to bring our various approaches into a coherent and concerted effort that puts people at the forefront of decision-making. I am hopeful that the work of the 66th session of the General Assembly has made some lasting contributions in this regard. With human security strengthened, I believe people can reach their full potential, thrive in the present, and build toward a future that is more peaceful and prosperous for all.[1]

Human Rights

The 66th session was a special year for human rights. It was special, extraordinary even, not only because millions of people around the world rose up to demand their basic human rights but also because of the unprecedented level of support the international community gave to these aspirations. The message from the General Assembly and the Human Rights Council—indeed from all parts of the United Nations— has been unequivocal: the popular will and legitimate demands of the people must be respected in accordance with the UN Charter and the Universal Declaration of Human Rights.

Of course, as we celebrate the recent human rights awakening, we must not forget that freedom from fear and from want remains a distant dream for far too many people around the world. Our challenge, as the international community, is to continue to push the boundaries of social, economic, political, and cultural freedoms so that ever more people throughout the world realize their human rights and fundamental freedoms. This is what the UN Charter demands of us: to achieve international cooperation in promoting and encouraging respect for "human rights and fundamental freedoms for all without distinction as to race, sex, language, or religion."[2]

As a relatively young entity of the UN system in its present form, the Human Rights Council has grown and developed considerably in responding to the needs for ensuring human rights all around the world. It has acted quickly and responded to many situations, and it has also promoted dialogue and cooperation among states on various human rights issues.

Since the Council's inception in 2006 (60/251), its foremost achievement has been the successful completion of the first cycle of the Universal Periodic Review (UPR) of all 193 UN member states on the basis of their human rights records and performance. The UPR provides an opportunity for a country to declare what actions it has taken to improve its human rights situations and to overcome challenges to the enjoyment of human rights. It includes a sharing of best human rights practices around the globe. Currently, no other mechanism of this kind exists.[3] The spirit of cooperation and, above all, the commitments displayed by the members to improve their human rights records is to be commended. I look forward to the second cycle of reviews and implementation of the commitments made.

I also note with appreciation that the Human Rights Council's deliberations, particularly in recent years, on collective and solidarity rights—such as the right to development, the right to food, the right to safe drinking water and sanitation, environmental rights, and even the right of peoples to peace—have very effectively engaged the international community's expectations.

Also worthy of special mention are the many panel discussions held on a broad range of human rights issues, forums that have drawn international attention to new and emerging issues and broadened international understanding of others. The active participation of UN entities and other international and regional organizations in these panel discussions—and more generally in the work of the Council—has contributed to human rights mainstreaming in the work of the United Nations as a whole.

I would also like to underscore the significant work carried out by the various special procedure mechanisms of the Council—the eyes and ears of the human rights system. They have a key role to play not only in human rights protection but also in broadening and advancing the understanding of key human rights issues.[4]

Under resolution 66/254, adopted February 23, 2012, the membership created the intergovernmental process of the General Assembly on strengthening and enhancing the effective functioning of the human rights treaty body system.[5] The process aims to strengthen the treaty bodies' capacity to assist state parties to relevant human rights treaties in meeting their relevant obligations, including through timely presentation and consideration of periodic reports.[6]

Disease Prevention and Control

All over the world, men and women are dying premature deaths. All over the world, men and women are dying preventable deaths. And all over the world, health care systems are overburdened and economic growth is curtailed because of the loss of healthy workers.

Let there be no doubt that noncommunicable diseases (NCDs) have reached epidemic proportions. Noncommunicable diseases are the most frequent cause of death worldwide. More than thirty-six million people die annually from noncommunicable diseases, making up 63 percent of global deaths. And these deaths could largely have been prevented. The impact of this loss, this tragedy, goes beyond individuals, beyond families. Noncommunicable diseases are altering demographics. They are stunting development. And they are impacting economic growth.

Since 2000, when member states at the World Health Assembly first committed to reducing the toll of premature mortality due to noncommunicable diseases, there have been important developments in our understanding of their causes and prevention. It has been recognized that people gain from primary health care services that are more responsive to early detection of cancers, diabetes, and heart disease. Likewise, people gain from public-sector policies that reduce their level of exposure to tobacco, unhealthy diets, physical inactivity, and alcohol abuse.

It has become unequivocally clear that "best buy" interventions that reduce the toll of NCD-related premature deaths are workable and affordable solutions. It is also evident that the most rapid improvements in public health are often realized from relatively inexpensive interventions that begin in childhood. And perhaps most significantly, it is now clear that, to move effectively to prevent and protect against noncommunicable diseases, governments must adopt approaches that go beyond just the health sectors.

In some wealthy nations, the health impact of noncommunicable diseases has been reduced by advocacy, community mobilization, health system organization, legislation, and regulation. We have seen less whole-of-government approaches in developing countries, and the experiences have been starkly different: premature deaths due to noncommunicable diseases among women range as low as 6 percent in high-income countries and as high as 58 percent in low-income countries. Among the many tragic consequences of such inequality is the impact on fulfilling the MDGs.[7]

On September 19, 2011, we held the first-ever General Assembly High-Level Meeting on the Prevention and Control of Non-communicable Diseases. Thanks to the engagement of member states, the UN system, in particular the World Health Organization (WHO), and civil society, NCDs were made a well-deserved priority on the global development agenda. A mandate was established, and clear responsibilities were delineated. Heads of state and government committed to developing national capacities for addressing NCDs and to strengthening their national NCD policies and plans.

The political declaration put forth at this meeting is a comprehensive document that lays concrete foundations for forward movement. But the true value of our work lies in its effective implementation.[8] Our main responsibility, I believe, is twofold: first, to support development of national capacities for addressing NCDs at the country level and to strengthen national NCD policies and plans; second, to assist the secretary-general in submitting options to the General Assembly for strengthening and facilitating multisectoral action for the prevention and control of NCDs through effective partnership.

In this context, I am pleased to note that the director-general of WHO and the administrator of UNDP addressed a joint letter to the UN Country Teams in March 2012, proposing that NCDs be integrated into the UN Development Assistance Framework (UNDAF) formulation and implementation. They asked that initial attention be paid to the countries where UNDAF rollouts are scheduled for 2012–2013. I was also very pleased to learn that the World Health Assembly decided last May to adopt a global target of 25 percent reduction in premature mortality from NCDs by the year 2025.

A number of significant global trends are contributing to the rise of NCDs in the developing world, among them aging populations, rapid unplanned urbanization, and the globalization of unhealthy lifestyles. With these challenges confronting us, we urgently need to realize the commitments included in the political declaration on NCDs. Let me highlight three areas that will require close attention as we engage in the implementation process.

First, multisectoral action against NCDs involves national authorities engaging across government sectors to reduce the exposure of populations to the risk factors for NCDs. For us to achieve ready health gains, we must work on influencing the public in sectors other than the health sector and beyond making changes in health policy alone. Various UN entities can mobilize sectors such as agriculture, communication, education, employment, environment, industry and trade, labor, transport, and urban planning toward a common agenda on NCDs.

Second, a more careful allocation and mobilization of resources will be essential for success. This includes supporting countries in exploring the opportunities for adequate, predictable, and sustained resources through domestic, bilateral, regional, and multilateral channels, including traditional and innovative financing mechanisms.

Third, we need to build a strategic alliance of UN agencies, funds, and programs that can advance these ambitious goals on NCDs. This alliance is most needed at this time to shape the development architecture through broad mobilization and engagement of stakeholders from governments, civil society, and the private sector. With the commitments and collaboration of the UN system and the excellent work of the WHO, we have the potential to save millions of lives and to assist millions more with prompt and appropriate care.[9]

Following the adoption of the Political Declaration on NCDs, we celebrated the 2011 South-South Awards on the theme "Digital Health for Digital Development." Only five years ago, who would have imagined that today a woman in sub-Saharan Africa could use a mobile phone to access health information on bringing her pregnancy safely to term? Or that today a young person in the Middle East could use a mobile phone to help manage diabetes?

The World Health Organization conducted a global survey in 2009 on the use of mobile technologies for health; the survey found that there is a groundswell of activity: 83 percent of member states reported offering at least one type of health service using mobile phones. Mobile phones are now the most widely used communication technology in the world, with more than 5.3 billion users. The number continues to grow at a very fast rate, especially in developing countries, providing unprecedented opportunities to apply mobile technology for health.

Many developing countries are well aware of the need to promote the potential of information and communication technologies in general, and mobile technologies in particular, for health. Many developing countries are already steaming ahead with digital health solutions that will serve as models for the entire world. In my view, digital health for digital development represents a fresh and invigorating approach to global health, a new movement of rising power with increasing diplomatic as well as economic clout.[10]

While I am optimistic about the progress in combating noncommunicable diseases, we must of course recognize that NCDs are not the only diseases that are preventable and deserving of the international community's attention. In 2011, at a high-level meeting of the General Assembly, member states unanimously adopted a historic Political Declaration on HIV and AIDs, which set clear targets to reduce the transmission of HIV. This commitment has inspired a new unity of purpose; a resolve to focus on results; and an opportunity to carve out clear roles for governments, donors, civil society, and the United Nations.

On June 11, 2012, we came together to review progress made since the adoption of the declaration. We were already achieving dramatic reductions in new infections in the hardest-hit countries and among young people worldwide. We were seeing a dramatic scale-up of treatments in low- and middle-income countries, from thousands to millions in just one decade.

The AIDS response has had a profound impact on human health and development—advancing the agendas of human rights, social justice, and gender equality; helping to build more inclusive societies; and moving science forward in the service of people. Yet critical challenges remain. HIV still disproportionately affects vulnerable populations. Populations at higher risk face additional stigmatization and discrimination, which only fuels the epidemic.

Funding is in decline, thereby diminishing the ability of the international community to sustain necessary progress. It is critical that we support the integration of HIV prevention, treatment, care, and support into relevant health and development programs. Such programs include those on sexual and reproductive health, maternal and child health, gender equality, noncommunicable disease responses, and the strengthening of health systems.

We must explore ways in which the scale-up of HIV prevention, treatment, care, and support may be leveraged not only to strengthen high-quality health services during specific periods of life—such as pregnancy and childhood—but to respond to a range of other health conditions and development challenges.

Achieving the ten targets set out in the 2011 Political Declaration is a worthy and achievable aim. But this is not a journey toward a single outcome. Built into the AIDS movement is the vast potential for global change that will be felt far beyond 2015. It is up to every single one of us—member states, civil society, private sector, and individuals—to work together, to step up the campaign, and to implement the commitments made for a better tomorrow.

Together we must act strategically and effectively to achieve the vision of a world with zero new HIV infections, zero discrimination, and zero AIDS-related deaths. This is a world I wish for us all.[11]

Rights of Persons with Disabilities and Disorders

On December 2, 2011, we commemorated both the International Day of Persons with Disabilities and the thirtieth anniversary of the United Nations International Year of Disabled Persons. An estimated 15 percent of the world's population has a disability. Over two-thirds of persons with disabilities live in developing countries.

It is no secret that men, women, and children with disabilities often face stigma and discrimination, including those who live in countries with high living standards. Many disabled persons cannot participate fully in their societies. Disabled populations are often the tragic consequence of war and conflict. Worldwide, the link between disability, poverty, and social exclusion is clear and direct.

Yet we have at our fingertips international human rights instruments that protect and promote the rights of persons with disabilities. The 1948 Universal Declaration of Human Rights reminds us that all human beings should enjoy the same rights and freedoms, without distinction of any kind. The United Nations Convention on the Rights of Persons with Disabilities, adopted in 2006 and entered into force in May 2008, covers the full spectrum of civil, cultural, economic, political, and social rights. It aims to promote, protect, and ensure the full and equal enjoyment of all rights and fundamental freedoms by persons with disabilities and to promote respect for their inherent dignity.[12]

This convention has been accepted by over half of all countries around the world, and we encourage the other half to commit to its ratification. But only if the convention is implemented at the national level can it have any positive impact on the lives of persons with disabilities. As is the case with all human rights treaties, the obligation for implementation falls on states.

But we all have a role to play. States are assisted through the oversight mechanisms provided by the convention and its Optional Protocol, and it is the UN's responsibility to make these function properly, to make them accessible to all persons affected by disabilities, and to disseminate them widely. This will require changes not only in law, policies, and programs but in attitudes as well. Change takes time and can be slow, but at a minimum, all persons with disabilities must enjoy equal respect and dignity—nothing less.[13]

On April 3, 2012, we marked the fifth World Autism Awareness Day with an event organized by His Excellency Dr. Abulkalam Abdul Momen, permanent representative of Bangladesh to the United Nations. On December 18, 2007, the United Nations General Assembly adopted resolution 62/139, declaring April 2 as the annual World Autism Awareness Day.[14] In celebration of the first World Autism Awareness Day on April 2, 2008, I was honored to ring the opening bell at the New York Stock Exchange (NYSE) along with the cofounder of Autism Speaks and other key supporters. This event is particularly close to my heart. Resolution 62/139 was presented by the State of Qatar, at the time when I was Qatar's ambassador to the United Nations. We worked hard for this

resolution, motivated by the strong belief that having an annual awareness day would shine a bright light on autism as a growing health concern. The resolution's adoption by consensus demonstrated that autism
is an issue that concerns us all—every nation.

World Autism Awareness Day is one of few health-specific United
Nations days. Resolution 62/139 encourages member states to take
measures to raise awareness about autism throughout society and to
encourage early diagnosis and early intervention. It further expresses a
deep concern at the prevalence and high rate of autism in children in all
regions of the world and the resulting developmental challenges.

Resolution 62/139 also recalls the Convention on the Rights of the
Child and the Convention on the Rights of Persons with Disabilities.
These resolutions affirm that children with disabilities should enjoy full
and decent lives in conditions that ensure dignity, promote self-reliance,
and ensure the full enjoyment of all human rights and fundamental
freedoms on an equal basis with other children.

In marking this annual event, each of us can help to increase and
develop global understanding of the autism challenge. We can also celebrate the unique talents and skills of persons with autism. By bringing
together member states and autism organizations all around the world,
we will give a voice to the millions of individuals worldwide who are
undiagnosed and looking for help.[15]

During my term, under the leadership of the Philippines and Tanzania, the Assembly demonstrated its strong commitment to the inclusion
of persons with disabilities in development by adopting a resolution to
hold a high-level meeting on disability and development. The meeting
was scheduled for September 23, 2013, the day before the beginning
of the General Debate, giving it maximum visibility and encouraging
member-state participation at the highest level.

It strikes me that "disability" contains a crucial word: "ability." Let us
reaffirm our commitment to building inclusive and empowering communities that harness the abilities of all and guarantee equal rights, freedoms, and dignity.[16]

Racism and Xenophobia

The people and the nations of the world make up one family, rich in diversity. It is our diversity that enriches humanity and steers progress. And it is through the celebration of this diversity, as well as through the promotion of tolerance and dispelling fears of the "other," that we will build a more peaceful world.

On September 22, 2011, we held a high-level meeting on one of the most critical global challenges of the twenty-first century: the continuing scourge of racism and xenophobia worldwide. It was also an opportunity to recommit to the full and effective implementation of the actions outlined in the Durban Declaration and Programme of Action (DDPA), which was adopted by consensus in 2001.[17]

Together with the outcome document of the Durban Review Conference, the DDPA is the most comprehensive framework for combating racism, racial discrimination, xenophobia, and related intolerance. It highlights issues faced by victims of racial discrimination, including people of African and Asian descent, migrants, refugees, and specific vulnerable groups such as indigenous peoples. It also emphasizes that we must remember the crimes and wrongs of the past, wherever and whenever they occurred. We must unequivocally condemn these racist tragedies and tell the truth about history. These are essential elements for international reconciliation and the creation of societies based on justice, equality, and solidarity.

Unfortunately, despite progress made since the DDPA was adopted in 2001, instances of xenophobia, racism, and intolerance have increased in severity and frequency. Racist attitudes and hate speech can be found in many countries, and the Internet provides a new vehicle for their proliferation. Despite concerted efforts, racist attitudes and racial discrimination continue to perpetuate deeply embedded social and economic disparities.

While many countries have come a long way in removing obstacles to the realization of the fundamental principles of equality and nondiscrimination, much more remains to be done. I encourage all countries, individually and collectively, to intensify efforts aimed at reducing instances of racism, racial discrimination, xenophobia, and related intolerance.

It is the responsibility of member states to take the necessary legislative measures to prevent the occurrence of discriminatory practices and to grant justice to the victims. Governments, in collaboration with other stakeholders including civil society and business, should intensify awareness-raising initiatives and enhance education in order to combat ignorance and effectively address the root causes of prejudice and negative stereotypes.[18]

It is vital that we go further to implement measures to counter intolerance and eradicate advocacy of hatred, incitement, and discrimination. It is vital that we do our utmost to promote and strengthen effective dialogue, which in turn increases understanding within and among communities and promotes social cohesion. And it is vital that we unite efforts and collaborate more intensively in order to effectively combat racism and other forms of discrimination.[19]

On October 13, 2011, I was honored to open the International Organization for Migration (IOM) meeting on the theme "Migration and Communication: Re-balancing Information Flows and Dialogue." Established in 1951, the IOM is the leading intergovernmental organization in the field of migration. It works closely with governmental, intergovernmental, and nongovernmental partners. With 151 member states, 12 observer states, and offices in more than one hundred countries, IOM seeks to promote humane and orderly migration for the benefit of all. It does so by providing services and advice to governments and migrants. It works in the four broad areas of migration management: migration and development; facilitating migration; regulating migration; and forced migration. IOM works to help ensure the orderly and humane management of migration, to promote international cooperation on migration issues, to assist in the search for practical solutions to migration problems, and to provide humanitarian assistance to migrants in need, including refugees and internally displaced people. The IOM Constitution recognizes the link between migration and development, as well as to the right of freedom of movement.[20]

Migration is undoubtedly one of the major global issues of the twenty-first century. Today, about 3 percent of the world's population lives outside their countries of birth. Accompanying this growing movement of people is increasing awareness that migration has important implications for development, both economic and social. Today, South-South migration has become as widespread as South-North migration. Most migration is actually taking place over short distances, to neighboring countries and within regions. New migration poles are emerging in Asia, Africa, and South America, in response to the labor demands created by an increasingly interdependent global economy. The largest shares of migrants to total population are not found in Europe or North America but rather in countries such as Arab states in the Gulf. In these countries, international migrants make up more than half of the working-age population.

Unfortunately, fear of the "other" has long plagued discussions around migration. And since the onset of the world financial and economic crisis, migrants have increasingly become the targets of racism and xenophobia. Dispelling myths and focusing on the contributions of migrants to development in countries of origin, transit, and destination is one way to rebalance the debate around migration.

The facts speak for themselves. While abroad, most international migrants transfer remittances that contribute to the well-being of families and communities of origin. In 2010, some US$325 billion was remitted to developing countries, far outpacing official development assistance. Migrants use these resources to improve the living standards of their families, often by paying for health and education. In the past few years, remarkable successes have been recorded in lowering the transfer cost of remittances. This has put more money in the hands of migrants and their families in their countries of origin, lifting many out of poverty. When they return home, international migrants bring their skills and expertise and global perspectives.

Migrant workers also make important contributions to economic growth in countries of destination. As entrepreneurs, migrants establish businesses and create jobs in the countries that host them. And in the face of aging populations in more developed countries, the role of migration cannot be overlooked.

A second approach to rebalancing the message is to ensure full respect for the rights of migrants in accordance with international human rights law and relevant instruments. The General Assembly has called on member states to effectively promote and protect the human rights and fundamental freedoms of all migrants, regardless of their migration status. This is especially crucial for women and children and for migrants in irregular situations.

Third, strengthening dialogue and information flows around migration requires greater coordination and cooperation at the global, regional, and bilateral levels. Migration is a global phenomenon that requires a global approach. If the full benefits of migration are to be leveraged, we need to work together, sharing information and best practices. The role of media in this endeavor cannot be underestimated.

Whereas migrants represent a state's newest arrivals, its longest inhabitants—indigenous peoples—are also frequent targets of racism and xenophobia. On May 17, 2012, we joined together to mark the fifth anniversary of the adoption of the UN Declaration on the Rights of Indigenous Peoples.[21] This declaration was the fruit of one of the longest and most complex standard-setting processes on which the United Nations ever embarked. With its adoption, humankind took a major step toward the realization of a just and equitable world, one that is founded on principles of equality, justice, and respect for diversity.

The UN Declaration on the Rights of Indigenous Peoples is a landmark in defending the individual and collective rights of indigenous peoples. The rights it enshrines constitute the minimum standards for the survival, dignity, and well-being of indigenous peoples. It has already inspired many positive changes in guaranteeing and protecting indigenous peoples' rights. In some countries, we have seen the creation of specialized institutions, the amendment of legislation and constitutions, the implementation of new policies and programs, judgments delivered by tribunals based on the declaration, and trainings on indigenous peoples' rights, among many other activities.

Yet we know that more remains to be done. A common concern of indigenous peoples is that governments need to involve and consult them when making decisions that affect them. To address this concern, the UN declaration clarifies international standards on the right of indigenous peoples to participate in decision-making on matters that affect their lives.

Access to financial and technical assistance from states and through international cooperation is critical to promoting and protecting the human rights of indigenous peoples, in accordance with the UN declaration. To facilitate this assistance, a number of mechanisms are in place, including the United Nations Voluntary Fund for indigenous populations, the Trust Fund for the Second International Decade of the World's Indigenous Peoples, and other trust funds by various United Nations agencies. The General Assembly has encouraged governments, intergovernmental organizations, and nongovernmental organizations —both private institutions and individuals—to continue to contribute to these funds.

Furthermore, in resolution 65/198, the UN General Assembly decided to organize a high-level plenary meeting of the General Assembly, to be known as the "World Conference on Indigenous Peoples" in 2014.[22] The World Conference will be an opportunity to share perspectives and best practices on the realization of the rights of indigenous peoples, with the United Nations Declaration on the Rights of Indigenous Peoples as the framework for discussions.

The preparation process for the World Conference is being conducted though partnership between member states and indigenous peoples, which have established a global coordinating group for the conference. I participated and monitored these preparations during my term as PGA and have high hopes that the work achieved there will carry the torch of this remarkable declaration and help to make its noble objectives a reality for indigenous peoples worldwide.[23]

Slavery and Human Trafficking

Sixty-five years ago, the General Assembly adopted the Universal Declaration of Human Rights. In doing so, it proclaimed that all humans are born free, that no one should be held in slavery or servitude, and that slavery and the slave trade should be prohibited in all their forms. Yet today, millions of people, the majority of them women and children, are victims of human trafficking.

Human trafficking is a global problem. It ranks as the world's third-most-profitable crime after illicit drug and arms trafficking. It is estimated that, across the globe, there are 2.4 million victims of human trafficking at any given time. Only one out of one hundred is ever rescued. No country is unaffected. We must do better.

In the 2005 World Summit outcome document, member states expressed grave concern about the negative effects on development, peace and security, and human rights posed by trafficking of human beings, as well as the increasing vulnerability of states to this crime. Member states recognized that trafficking in persons continues to pose a serious challenge to humanity and requires a concerted international response.

Human trafficking also impacts our ability to fulfill the Millennium Development Goals, particularly MDG 8, "Develop a Global Partnership for Development." The root causes of child trafficking lie in underdevelopment.

A global partnership aimed at fostering good governance, debt relief, and official development assistance can contribute to reducing poverty and corruption, limiting the supply and demand for trafficking.

Cross-border and international cooperation are also necessary to monitor and stop child trafficking.

I am proud to be one of the original members of the Group of Friends United Against Human Trafficking. In 2010, the group turned the concerns of member states into concrete action by negotiating and passing by consensus a comprehensive UN Global Plan of Action to Combat Trafficking in Persons.[24] A Trust Fund for Victims was established by the General Assembly, and I am pleased to see that the United Nations Office on Drugs and Crime (UNODC) has already begun to establish a small grants facility to start distributing funds. In 2012, UNODC will publish its biennial global report on trafficking in persons, thanks to the efforts of the Group of Friends.

Although human trafficking takes place in the dark margins of our societies, we must not ignore its presence. All nations must work together to end this assault on human dignity. We must prosecute and punish the criminals involved and protect and reintegrate the victims into their communities. We must spur governments and all members of society into action to reduce the vulnerability of victims and to increase the consequences for traffickers.[25]

Toward this end, we held an important interactive dialogue on April 3, 2012, on the theme "Fighting Human Trafficking: Partnership and Innovation to End Violence against Women and Girls." The majority of persons trafficked are the weakest and most vulnerable members of society: children, women, and migrants. They are subject to forced labor, domestic servitude, and sexual exploitation in every country and every region of the world.

In 2003, the United Nations adopted a zero-tolerance policy with the title "Special Measures for Protection from Sexual Exploitation and Sexual Abuse."[26] This policy applies to tens of thousands of uniformed UN personnel—troops, military observers, and police. It also applies to UN international and national staff members, contractors, consultants, and UN volunteers serving in peacekeeping and humanitarian missions.

An international conference on the theme "Trafficking in Women and Girls: Meeting the Challenges Together" was held at UN Headquarters in March 2007. With its emphasis on multistakeholder participation, the event was the first to call for a comprehensive and coordinated response to counter human trafficking. The interactive dialogue in April 2012 was the five-year follow-up to that 2007 conference and aimed to express solidarity with victims and to unite member states to end this crime for those who suffer now and for all future generations.

Children born today, particularly girls, should not have to face the possibility of being forced into this modern form of slavery tomorrow. I urge everyone—whether an individual, an organization, or a state—to speak out on this issue. We have to redouble our efforts to ensure that concrete and concerted action upholds basic rights and freedoms for all, bringing an end to this appalling crime.[27]

While we work to combat the shameful practice of slavery in all its current forms, we must also remember its countless historical victims. On March 23, 2012, I presided over a special meeting of the General Assembly on the occasion of the International Day of Remembrance of the Victims of Slavery and the Transatlantic Slave Trade, and on May 15, 2012, we held a concert "Honouring the Heroes, Resisters and Survivors of Slavery."

At both events, we saluted the courage of the brave men and women who rebelled against the cruel and brutal practice of slavery and who, in doing so, regained their spirit and their independence, both during slavery and in its aftermath. We collectively reaffirmed the commitment of the international community to preventing such suffering from occurring again.

Over a period of four hundred years, millions of our African brothers and sisters were forcibly removed from their homes and cast into a lifetime of servitude, torment, and despair. The terrible effects of slavery and the slave trade are still felt to this day. They have devastated continents and countries.

As PGA, I lent my support to plans for the creation of a Permanent

Memorial to Honor the Victims of Slavery at UN Headquarters. Such a memorial would be a lasting tribute to one of the most tragic chapters in the history of humankind.[28] Let us learn from the horrors and sacrifices of the past and ensure through concrete actions and results that slavery in all its forms is forever eliminated.[29]

Crime Prevention and Security

On April 23, 2012, we held the 21st Session of the Commission on Crime Prevention and Criminal Justice. Worldwide, we are witnessing the scourge of transnational organized crime undermining the rule of law, economic development, and human rights. It is not simply the problem of certain communities or law enforcement agencies; it has evolved into a far wider and more sophisticated challenge. Over time, criminal arteries around the world have hardened into permanent networks for the illicit drug trade, human trafficking, arms smuggling, money laundering, and piracy.

Together, these crimes generate enormous profits every year: not in the millions, not in the billions, but in the *trillions* of dollars. The profits wash through the world's financial systems, undermining legitimate economies through the corruption of political processes and law enforcement agencies. The price is paid by individuals, families, and communities, in countries that are already fragile and vulnerable.

Crime is an infection. While it spreads to weak and strong alike, it is fragile or vulnerable states that lack the strength to fight off the contamination. Our collective challenge is to find solutions. We can no longer afford to think in terms of the local and the regional. Crime transcends these borders and spans the planet, and so must our responses. We must focus our efforts to promote security and justice, the rule of law, and public institutions that are fully functioning. Knowledge must become our touchstone.

Crime is fast moving, intelligent, and interconnected. To stop it, we need to share information in real time and to build a truly united global partnership. At the center of our efforts to address this critical issue is the Task Force on Organized Crime and Drug Trafficking, jointly chaired by UNODC and the Department of Political Affairs (DPA). Established in 2011 by the secretary-general, the Task Force seeks to craft effective and efficient responses to crime in accordance with the UN Convention Against Illicit Traffic in Narcotic Drugs and Psychotropic Substances, the UN Convention on Transnational Crime and its protocols, and the UN Convention Against Corruption. It is cochaired by the United Nations Office on Drugs and Crime and the United Nations Department of Political Affairs and composed of the Department for Peacekeeping Operations, the United Nations Development Programme (UNDP), the Department of Political Affairs, the Peacebuilding Support Office, the Office of the High Commissioner for Human Rights (OHCHR), the United Nations Children's Fund (UNICEF), UN-Women, and the World Bank.[30]

Under my presidency, the General Assembly dedicated considerable time and energy to the discussion of transnational organized crime and adopted numerous resolutions on crime: on combating the harmful effects of illicit financial flows resulting from criminal activities; strengthening crime prevention and criminal justice responses to protect cultural property, especially with regard to its trafficking; and strengthening the United Nations crime prevention and criminal justice program, in particular, its technical cooperation capacity.

We need to create a seamless thread connecting these resolutions to the work carried out by the Crime Commission and to the activities of the United Nations and member states on the ground. As we look forward to the thirteenth UN Congress on Crime Prevention and Criminal Justice hosted by Qatar in 2015, we must begin to set in motion our integrated efforts and to build the momentum to eradicate these crimes once and for all.[31]

In keeping with this goal, on May 16, 2012, we held a debate of the General Assembly on the theme "Security in Central America as a Regional and Global Challenge: How to Improve and Implement the

Central American Security Strategy." Countries in Central America are facing a tide of violence, born of transnational organized crime and drug trafficking. Human trafficking, migrant smuggling, and kidnapping have also attached themselves to the underbellies of Central American societies.

Highly sophisticated criminal threats in the region are eroding economic development, corrupting legal and political processes, and undermining public confidence. In a word, these threats risk unraveling gains made in development in the region and leading to social and political upheaval. The General Assembly debate engaged leaders, the media, and civil society about how best to achieve security in Central America.

Adopted at the meeting of the heads of state of Central America in June 2011, the "Regional Security Strategy for Central America" is a comprehensive step forward in efforts to answer this question. It seeks to create a region that is "safe, in peace, with freedom, democracy and development."[32] The strategy has received broad endorsement from the Group of Friends of the Conference, including UNODC, UNDP, the World Bank, and other international organizations.

Security in Central America is a concern not only for the Central American region. Many countries and regions outside Central America are also affected—directly or indirectly—by regional events.[33] Distinguished opening speakers, panelists, and participants at the thematic debate shared helpful insight into the challenges that face not only Central America but also Africa and Europe.

Speakers agreed that the increasingly global problem of organized crime requires an international response that is closely aligned with existing regional and interregional cooperation initiatives. Our response should be carefully coordinated with our partners, particularly national and local leadership, to ensure that our assistance is applicable to the specific context. We should also involve the private sector and local communities.

Member states also called for "shared but differentiated" responsibility among all affected countries to fight impunity. Transit countries bear a particular burden: they are the source of neither the demand nor the supply, but they often suffer from drug-related violence in their territories. UN member states have worked tirelessly over the past two decades to pass crime prevention resolutions and to establish a legal framework to prevent and fight international crime, including corruption. I would encourage member states that have not yet done so to become parties to relevant UN conventions. States can also strengthen national laws and procedures against organized crime and corruption and can work to harmonize these with international law.[34]

Peacekeeping and the Responsibility to Protect

The presence of the UN on the ground helps stop the escalation of confrontations, saving the lives of countless men, women, and children worldwide. It paves the way for the peaceful settlement of disputes. It helps rebuild communities after conflicts and improves the lives of populations, including the most vulnerable.

None of this could be achieved without the tireless work of our peacekeepers—military, police, and civilians—serving under the UN flag. Today, UN peacekeeping faces many trials, both at Headquarters and around the world.

From March 2010 until November 2011, 195 of our UN colleagues gave their lives in service to our organization: peacekeepers in Darfur, trying to keep internally displaced persons (IDPs) safe; staff in Abuja, victims of terrorism; colleagues in Kinshasa, traveling by plane. On November 21, 2011, we gathered to pay tribute and to honor the memory of these brave and beloved friends and colleagues. I would like to express my deepest respect and gratitude to those who have served the UN around the world—far from their countries and loved ones—and who have made the ultimate sacrifice. Their work and dedication underpins the core mission of the United Nations: the promotion of peace, security, and prosperity worldwide.

From Congo to Kosovo, from Haiti to Afghanistan, for more than half a century, the men and women of the UN have never hesitated to move into some of the world's most challenging environments. I commend the Secretariat's work in pressing forward the implementation of the safety and security policies and procedures established through the Inter-agency Security Management Network. Full implementation across all missions will allow better assessment of the risks associated with UN operations in the field and, thereby, lead to better operational decision-making.[35]

It must also be acknowledged that the complexity of mandates for peacekeeping operations has greatly increased over the years. Missions are charged not only with supporting the implementation of comprehensive peace accords but also with transitional administration. Many missions are also largely focused on the physical protection of civilians. This requires a renewed global partnership among all stakeholders, in particular host countries, troop contributors, regional organizations, and UN staff.

On February 21, 2012, I addressed the opening session of the Special Committee on Peacekeeping Operations. The contributions of this committee stand at the core of the United Nations mission: the promotion of peace, security, and prosperity worldwide.

Mandates for peacekeeping operations are discussed and decided by the Security Council. However, decisions on financing, on elaborating policies and guidelines, and on reviewing their implementation are made by the Fourth and the Fifth Committees and through the work of this Special Committee, under the authority of the General Assembly and its 193 members. The contributions of both the Security Council and the Assembly are crucial for the acceptance and strengthening of our actions.

We should also spare no effort in ensuring that our missions have the level of resources—human and material—that provide the best possible levels for a successful implementation of their mandates. I hope that the Special Committee will continue to advance the discussions on these topics, including the improvements of its own working methods.

At the same time, we must maximize the use of national capacities from the beginning. Yet this will not be possible without providing rapid, effective international civilian assistance. Let me underscore, once again, that the safety and security of UN personnel—civilian and uniformed—must be a top priority for all involved: the General Assembly, the Security Council, and the Secretariat. To this end, we must work closely with host countries, which bear the primary responsibility for safety and security in their respective territories.[36]

On March 23, 2012, we held a high-level briefing on the theme "Broadening the Concept of Peacekeeping: The Contribution of Civil Society to the Unarmed Protection of Civilians." The concept of unarmed protection of civilians was deliberated among member states with different approaches.

Ever more, we see civil society actors supporting—directly or indirectly—the UN's efforts to protect people in need. Through their broad experience, civil society actors have developed and implemented innovative, local methods for protecting civilians, without relying on the use of force on the ground.

As past experiences have taught us, every conflict or dispute is distinct. Each one requires careful attention and the most appropriate tools. But no single actor can do it alone. Legitimacy, good governance, good coordination, and reaffirming sovereignty, territorial integrity, and national ownership are all interlinked elements to make the task a success.

In some cases, civil society organizations act in a more informal, timely, and flexible way than state actors or international organizations can. The cases of Libya and Syria are good examples. Territories under occupation also offer similar experiences. This advantage is to be benefited from. The earlier the preventive action, the more cost-effective it is likely to be as well.[37]

As discussed in chapter 1, heads of state and government, gathered at the United Nations for the 2005 World Summit, adopted the concept of the responsibility to protect (R2P) with the aim of guarding populations against genocide, war crimes, ethnic cleansing, and crimes against humanity. This commitment was compelled, in part, by recent failures of the international community to prevent the tragedies of genocide and war crimes in some parts of the world, namely, Srebrenica, Rwanda, and Kosovo.

The governments of the world not only renewed their commitment to protecting their own populations but also vowed to respond collectively when confronted with clear cases of governments being unable or unwilling to protect their citizens from mass atrocities. Heads of state and government also requested that the General Assembly keep the concept of the responsibility to protect under continued consideration.

Since 2009, we have therefore held annual, informal, interactive dialogues with the objective of further developing different aspects of this concept. Every one of these annual discussions has been supported by a report of the secretary-general, prepared for the consideration of the General Assembly. On September 5, 2012, I had the pleasure of presiding over that year's interactive dialogue on R2P.

In the secretary-general's first report, in 2009, he outlined a strategy for the implementation of the responsibility to protect concept. Since then, the international community has made some progress toward refining the concept, strengthening partnerships, and sharpening the tools for its implementation. However, some aspects of the concept could still benefit from further refinement.

We must acknowledge that controversy still exists over selectivity and timing of response, monitoring of Security Council resolutions, and other matters raised in relation to implementation and necessary action. These are legitimate concerns. The role of the UN is not to supplant or replace the state in meeting its legal obligation to protect. The international community can only act in the event that a state "manifestly fails" to protect its citizens.

In the 2012 report, the secretary-general encouraged us to pay particular attention to the close relationship between prevention and response, as well as the range of tools available, including noncoercive measures, plus partnerships for implementation. I again commend Secretary-General Ban Ki-moon for designating 2012 the Year of Prevention. Prevention is the first line of defense against genocide, war crimes, ethnic cleansing, and crimes against humanity.

The use of force—under chapter 7 of the United Nations Charter— must be a measure of last resort, to be carried out in a proportional manner, bearing in mind the balance of consequences. The valuable Brazilian initiative "Responsibility while Protecting" calls on international actors to act responsibly during every stage of the implementation of this concept.

I have no doubt that the committed engagement of the UN will help to ensure the credible, legitimate, and timely protection of populations from genocide, war crimes, ethnic cleansing, and crimes against humanity.[38]

Crisis in Syria

In a report published November 23, 2011, the Independent International Commission of Inquiry on the Syrian Arab Republic indicated that gross and systematic violations of human rights had been committed by the Syrian authorities and members of the Syrian military and security forces in different locations in the Syrian Arab Republic. Already in November 2011, the report stated that crimes against humanity had been committed in Syria.

The Syrian authorities refused to cooperate with the Commission of Inquiry or even to give it access to the Syrian territory. The League of Arab States took strong initiatives to promote a peaceful solution to the Syrian crisis, including sending an observer mission, which had to be suspended on January 28, 2012, due to the critical deterioration of the situation and the continued use of violence.

The Arab League then adopted a new plan to resolve the Syrian crisis, which the Security Council has so far been unable to support through adoption of a resolution. The longer the Security Council remains divided in adopting a position on developments in Syria, the more difficult the situation becomes, with more Syrians being killed daily.

I am deeply concerned about the ongoing violence in Syria. As president of the General Assembly, it was also my responsibility to let the members of the United Nations express their views on the situation. On February 13, 2012, at the Plenary Meeting of the General Assembly, I asked the high commissioner for human rights, Mrs. Navi Pillay, to brief us on developments since the report was received in November.[39] An overwhelming number of member states expressed their concern about the ongoing violence in Syria and the need to end the killings and other human rights violations.

With this momentum, resolution 66/253 was adopted by the General Assembly on February 16 with a majority of 137 votes in favor. This resolution endorses the Arab League initiative and acknowledges the violations perpetrated against civilians by the Syrian government. According to the resolution, former United Nations secretary-general Mr. Kofi Annan was appointed as joint special envoy to Syria for the UN and League of Arab States.

Later that month, I traveled to Geneva, Switzerland, to attend the nineteenth session of the Human Rights Council. I commended the Council for its courageous action in responding to human rights situations worldwide—particularly in Syria, on which the Council had already held three special sessions. Before arriving in Geneva, I visited a number of countries for deliberations with heads of state and governments. The Syrian crisis was of the utmost concern to them all due to its flagrant violations against civilians.[40]

The Geneva meeting took place at a crucial moment for Syria. The situation on the ground had continued to deteriorate with the use of tanks, rockets, and artillery by the Syrian authorities against civilians. The lack of medical supplies was also a major concern. I renewed the call for the high commissioner of human rights, the president of the Human Rights Council, the Security Council, and the General Assembly to act as one to face this crisis and end it with the least loss of life possible.[41]

On April 5, I invited Mr. Annan to brief the General Assembly in his role as special envoy to Syria for the UN and League of Arab States. An agreement had been reached between Mr. Annan and the Syrian government on a six-point plan of action that was to be implemented by April 10.[42] The Security Council adopted resolutions 2042 and 2043, endorsing the six-point plan and establishing the United Nations Supervision Mission in Syria (UNSMIS), which was promptly deployed.[43]

Tragically, the Syrian regime neglected to implement the six-point plan, and the number of casualties continued to mount. On May 25 and 26, atrocities were committed in the region of El-Houleh, and on June 6, in Al-Qoubeir, west of Hama. Dozens of men, women, and young children were killed; hundreds more were wounded. Civilians were severely abused and deliberately shot at close range by pro-regime elements. Government artillery and tanks shelled residential neighborhoods.

The high commissioner for human rights repeatedly encouraged the Security Council to refer the situation in Syria to the International Criminal Court. Such crimes against humanity require a transparent, independent, and impartial international investigation. Those responsible must be held accountable.

On June 7, we held another Plenary Session of the General Assembly on events in the Syrian Arab Republic. I urged all member states to unite in cooperating with the joint special envoy and to impress on the Syrian government and all parties the need for a cessation of violence in all its forms and for a rapid and peaceful solution to the situation. We observed a minute of silence to mourn those who had lost their lives in this crisis.[44]

In the face of escalating violence in Syria, the General Assembly met on the situation again on August 3. Syrian government forces had intensified their military operations against areas presumed to be strongholds of antigovernment armed groups, in particular the cities of Damascus and Aleppo. Gross violations of human rights were occurring daily. There were horrifying reports about mass killings, rape, extrajudicial executions, torture, and deliberate targeting of civilians.

I expressed my deep regret that the Security Council had again been unable to unite and take collective action to put an end to this appalling crisis. The deadlock in the Security Council sends the wrong signal to all parties in the Syrian conflict. It was also discouraging to learn of Mr. Annan's intention not to renew his mandate when it expired at the end of August.[45]

On September 4, 2012, as the General Assembly again gathered to discuss the situation, millions of Syrians remained in a state of huge uncertainty and fear of death in their own country. The government of President Bashar al-Assad had turned its guns against its own people in total disregard of international norms and international commitments. Hundreds of thousands of defenseless Syrians had fled their homes to seek security and refuge in neighboring countries. Those who could not leave had been left stranded and displaced in schools and public buildings. UN agencies estimated that some 2.5 million Syrians were in urgent need of humanitarian assistance at that very moment.

Finally, the Security Council agreed to the creation of a liaison office to support international efforts for a political solution. Consensus on the need to keep a UN presence in Damascus was a crucial step toward peace. Another positive development was the appointment of the widely respected Algerian diplomat His Excellency Mr. Lakhdar Brahimi as the new joint special representative of the UN and the League of Arab States. I thanked Mr. Brahimi for accepting this critical and challenging assignment and extended to him my best wishes and full support.

At the end of the 66th session, though the crisis in Syria was ongoing, I was proud that the United Nations General Assembly had chosen not to stay silent. We passed relevant and important General Assembly resolutions in February, June, and August, strongly condemning the continued widespread and systematic violations of human rights by the Syrian authorities. We repeatedly called on the Syrian government to end the killings of its own people. We repeatedly called for an all-inclusive, Syrian-led political process.

Our calls still stand. The killings must stop now. The gross human rights violations and the violations of international humanitarian law must end. And those who commit these atrocities must be brought to justice. The UN Charter places a responsibility on the General Assembly to take steps, where necessary, to promote and ensure international peace and security. The General Assembly has demonstrated its role, relevance, and legitimacy in this regard. I commend and thank member states and distinguished delegates of the Assembly for the support they gave me, as president of the General Assembly, on this issue.[46]

Combating Terrorism

Our world is afflicted by the menace of terrorism. Terrorists are committed to indiscriminate violence and use fear and brutality rather than peaceful means toward achieving their goals. Their methods have no basis or support in any faith, any national conscience, or in any part of our global civilization. Acts of terrorism undermine the very principles and ideals on which the UN was founded, and they challenge national efforts toward security and prosperity.

All member states have recognized the threat presented by terrorism and look to the General Assembly as an important venue for establishing partnerships between relevant stakeholders, sharing knowledge, and of course developing international norms on counterterrorism. Notably, the United Nations Global Counter-Terrorism Strategy, adopted by consensus, is a unique achievement of the international community against terrorism. The strategy is a comprehensive and preventive approach that provides an integrated framework for member states to follow.[47]

On September 19, 2011, the secretary-general convened a Symposium on International Counter-Terrorism Cooperation, reminding member states that we can only counter and defeat this threat if we work together and act on our collective commitment to implement the Global Strategy. The symposium also provided an opportunity to recommend measures to cover gaps in our counterterrorism efforts, be they in the domains of law enforcement, capacity building, or human rights. It is only through focused, interactive discussion that we can achieve this objective.[48]

On June 27, 2012, I chaired a seminar on the theme "Dialogue, Understanding and Countering the Appeal of Terrorism," organized in cooperation with the UN Inter-regional Crime and Justice Research Institute (UNICRI) and the Counter-Terrorism Implementation Task Force (CTITF). Their work has been key in our efforts to identify and apply concrete steps toward countering the appeal of terrorism.

It has become clear that security, law enforcement, and judicial measures alone are not enough to combat the spread of terrorism and to prevent the radicalization of segments of the population, particularly youth. To counter the appeal of terrorism effectively, we must implement practical and sustainable measures that are customized to local and regional conditions. We cannot have a "one size fits all" approach.

First, we need to develop a better and deeper understanding of how to combat intolerance, ideological extremism, social marginalization, and discrimination against minority communities. These are some of the factors that lead to radicalization. By considering them, we can be in a better position to identify the best policies for addressing these challenges successfully. We must also address the related issues of deradicalization and rehabilitation in prison settings.

Second, by promoting dialogue, tolerance, and understanding among civilizations, cultures, peoples, and religions, we can help promote mutual respect and foster more open and inclusive societies. In this way, we can succeed by using obligations under national and international laws to prohibit and prevent incitement to commit terrorist acts. We must also work to effectively combat the defamation of all religions and incitement to religious hatred.

Through appropriate education and the necessary political will, we can remove the conditions that are conducive to the spread of terrorism. We should also make progress by exchanging best practices in enhancing dialogue in order to combat violent extremism. We should draw lessons from successful educational programs so we can become more conversant with the challenges of countering the use of the Internet for terrorist purposes. And in these efforts, we must always listen to voices of the victims.

We have an opportunity to defeat the extremist narrative, and we can stop the violence and bloodshed that often result from such extremism.[49] The June seminar contributed greatly toward identifying some concrete methods to do so. Participants also noted that these practices need to be implemented effectively, consistently, and equitably across communities in order to be fruitful.

We have a number of institutions within the United Nations system that member states can benefit from in this effort. The CTITF is a particularly useful platform that links the worth of dialogue and understanding to the broader struggle against terrorism. In this regard, the UN Alliance of Civilizations can play an important role to enhance dialogue and mutual understanding among people. I urge all states to consider taking advantage of these UN organs and their respective activities in order to make a difference on the ground.[50]

Disarmament and Nuclear Safety

The Fukushima Daiichi disaster in March 2011 was a loud global wake-up call. It was a stark reminder that ensuring nuclear safety requires the maintenance of the highest nuclear safety and security standards, as well as long-term disaster preparedness and strong international cooperation.

When one of the world's best-prepared countries can experience such a large-scale nuclear accident, it is all too clear that we must continue to evolve our thinking and practices for the safe and secure operation of nuclear facilities worldwide. I commend the prompt action by the International Atomic Energy Agency in responding to the crisis. I also commend the organization's convening of the IAEA Ministerial Conference on Nuclear Safety in June 2011 and its adoption of the IAEA Action Plan on Nuclear Safety. The significance of this Action Plan cannot be underestimated, as it charts the way forward for an effective and reliable global nuclear safety framework.[51]

On September 22, 2011, the secretary-general convened a High-Level Meeting on Nuclear Safety and Security as part of his five-point initiative announced in Kiev in April. I also wish to commend the secretary-general for launching, in May 2011, the UN system-wide study on the implications of the accident at the Fukushima Daiichi nuclear power plant. Relevant international organizations made valuable contributions to the preparation of the system-wide study.

The high-level meeting in September reinforced that the growing interest in nuclear energy is largely a product of global energy demands and concerns over energy security. Nuclear technologies also have important applications in fields such as health, food and agriculture, the environment, and water resources. Safe and efficient use of nuclear energy can advance the well-being of states and their peoples and help to achieve key MDGs. Serious examination of safe and efficient use of nuclear energy must thus consider closely related issues, including advancing nuclear disarmament and nuclear nonproliferation goals, the prevention of nuclear terrorism, and others.

The meeting represented a valuable opportunity to advance our international determination to review, strengthen, and upgrade, as necessary, nuclear safety standards, practices, and capabilities to the highest possible levels. I pledged to continue working with both the Secretariat and member states to follow up on efforts to ensure that the United Nations and its relevant bodies and specialized agencies continue to play an effective role in this important area.[52] Indeed, my term as PGA included a notably busy agenda of disarmament and arms-control meetings. These included the United Nations Conference on the Arms Trade Treaty, the Review Conference of the UN Program of Action on Small Arms and Light Weapons, the First Preparatory Committee for the 2015 Review Conference of the Treaty on the Non-Proliferation of Nuclear Weapons, and several others.[53]

On April 2, 2012, I attended the opening of the 2012 session of the

United Nations Disarmament Commission (UNDC), as the commission began a new three-year cycle. We acknowledged that the disarmament machinery of the UN is facing serious challenges imposed by a lack of political will and a growing resistance to initiative and compromise that has brought the work of both the UNDC and the Conference on Disarmament to a stalemate for over a decade. For the twelfth consecutive year, member states could not arrive at an agreement over an outcome for the session in 2011. I thanked the UNDC for facing this serious challenge and asked its members to exert every effort required to seize the opportunity present at the current session.[54]

On May 15, 2012, I addressed the Conference on Disarmament (CD). Since its establishment as a result of the first Special Session of the United Nations General Assembly devoted to Disarmament (SSOD1) held in 1978, the Conference on Disarmament remains the single multilateral disarmament-negotiating forum of the international community. Its terms of reference include practically all multilateral arms control and disarmament problems. Currently, the CD focuses on the following issues: cessation of the nuclear arms race and nuclear disarmament; prevention of nuclear war; prevention of an arms race in outer space; effective international arrangements to assure non-nuclear-weapon states against the use or threat of use of nuclear weapons; new types of weapons of mass destruction and new systems of such weapons; comprehensive program of disarmament; and transparency in armaments. The CD comprises sixty-five countries and meets annually. Over its history, the CD has produced landmark disarmament instruments including the Treaty on the Non-Proliferation of Nuclear Weapons, the Chemical Weapons Convention, and the Comprehensive Nuclear-Test-Ban Treaty.[55]

In the General Assembly's resolutions 65/93 in 2010 and 66/420 in 2011 on "revitalizing the work of the conference on disarmament" and taking forward multilateral disarmament negotiations, it recognized that although the political will to advance the disarmament agenda has been strengthened in recent years, the CD has failed to make substantive progress for well over a decade.[56] As a result, the credibility of this crucially important body is at a high risk.

On the other hand, the years from 2010 to 2012 have witnessed important progress on bilateral, regional, and multilateral levels. For example, the Russian Federation and the United States negotiated and concluded a new treaty on the reduction and limitation of strategic offensive arms. Furthermore, the States Parties to the Treaty on the Non-Proliferation of Nuclear Weapons (NPT) had a successful review conference in 2010 with concrete and promising steps taken on the question of establishing a nuclear-weapon-free zone in the Middle East—an item on the agenda of the UN General Assembly for decades.

These developments demonstrate progress and make a positive impact on the global security environment. But they have been achieved in disconnect from the Conference on Disarmament. The Conference on Disarmament must do its part to advance the international agenda through its invaluable work. At the First Committee Session in October 2011, intensive discussions among delegations clearly revealed that revitalizing the disarmament machinery, including in particular the Conference on Disarmament, was an emerging and ever-more-pressing priority.

The future of the Conference on Disarmament is in its member states' hands. First and foremost, the CD must adopt a program of work without delay. A number of very constructive proposals have been put forward, and delegations should allow the president of the CD to lead this effort in serious and inclusive consultations over a draft program that is consensual and realistic, if not necessarily ideal. The perfect has been the enemy of the good for too long.[57]

Coupled with efforts aimed at disarmament, there has been half a century of extensive international efforts aimed at banning nuclear test explosions. Indeed, much has been achieved. The Comprehensive Nuclear-Test-Ban Treaty (CTBT) represents a culmination of those efforts, particularly with the completion of a significant portion of the treaty's global verification infrastructure.[58]

The CTBT is upholding the international norm against nuclear testing. It has also established a verification regime that continues to empower signatory states with advanced technical capabilities in the analysis of data obtained from verification stations across the globe. With such capabilities, signatories to the CTBT are able to detect, in a timely and effective manner, any nuclear test explosions, wherever they occur. The deterrence effect that this represents has kept a tight lid on nuclear testing for over a decade, with few known exceptions.

The peaceful applications of verification technologies also represent a valuable facet of the importance of the system. Over US$1 billion of international funding has been invested in the establishment and operation of the CTBT's verification system. This investment is proving most valuable for an extremely important cause that is connected almost directly to the very survival of the human race.

While much has been achieved to bring us closer to a universally effective, legally binding comprehensive nuclear test ban, much remains to be done. Stronger political commitment and true leadership are needed today more than ever. In proposing the initial draft of the General Assembly consensus resolution 64/35, Kazakhstan provided a noteworthy example that allowed the General Assembly to establish August 29 of each year as an International Day against Nuclear Tests.[59] (Kazakhstan had also unilaterally closed down the Semipalatinsk nuclear test site more than a decade earlier.)

We observed this occasion in 2012 with Ambassador Susan Burk, special representative of the president of the United States for nuclear nonproliferation, who came from Washington, D.C., to support the cause and share her profound experiences with us on a range of extremely important topics. We also heard from distinguished speakers including Mr. Timur Zhantikin, chairman of the Atomic Energy Agency of the Republic of Kazakhstan. It is my hope that the efforts of CTBT will continue and will gradually succeed in bringing us closer to achieving our collective objective, that is, a world where all nations can live in peace and stability without the looming threat and danger of nuclear destruction.[60]

On August 30, 2012, I addressed the sixteenth summit of the Non-Aligned Movement in Tehran, Iran. The Non-Aligned Movement (NAM) is a group of states which are not formally aligned with or against any major power bloc. Currently the NAM has 113 members and 17 observer countries. The first Conference of Non-Aligned Heads of State, at which 25 countries were represented, was convened at Belgrade in September 1961 out of concern that an accelerating arms race might result in war between the Soviet Union and the United States.[61]

The importance of resolving the Iranian nuclear issue by peaceful means and in accordance with international law cannot be overestimated. Iran has the right, just as other state parties to the Treaty on the Non-Proliferation of Nuclear Weapons, to use nuclear energy for peaceful purposes, in accordance with international law, which regulates this right and governs the obligations associated with it. We need good faith to be demonstrated in order to build confidence between all the regional and international parties on this issue.

It is of the utmost importance that the security and stability of the Gulf region should be maintained if the stability of the world as a whole is to be preserved. Commitment by the Gulf states to the principle of good-neighborliness will strengthen the maintenance of international peace and security. The Non-Aligned Movement in all its variety and with all its political weight is a fundamental partner in strengthening and activating efforts to achieve our lofty goal of making the world more secure and prosperous.[62]

While nuclear safety and disarmament remain top priorities of the General Assembly, we are also deeply concerned with the illicit manufacture, transfer, and circulation of small arms and light weapons and the consequences for the well-being of millions of people around the world. In 2001, the Assembly urgently adopted the Programme of Action to Prevent, Combat and Eradicate the Illicit Trade in Small Arms and Light Weapons in All Its Aspects.[63] Our commitment represented a landmark consensus against the trafficking of small arms, and it gave us what turned out to be an essential tool, on the national, regional, and international levels.

On August 27, 2012, we gathered for the second review conference to mark that consensus and to review our progress in realizing our commitments. Although the uncontrolled spread of small arms and light weapons in the illicit market continues to pose a serious threat to global peace and security, it was encouraging to see how much progress we had achieved since the adoption of the Programme of Action in 2001.

Various initiatives, including those of the United Nations, other international, regional, and subregional organizations, as well as of civil society organizations, have contributed to increased awareness and implementation of activities at all levels. A growing majority of states not only have reported on the Programme of Action's implementation but have also advanced legislation to restrict the flow of illicit small arms and light weapons in their territories. Many have also established national coordinating bodies and extended their help to other states in need of assistance for capacity building in the implementation of the program.

Despite all the progress achieved, small arms and light weapons outside government control continue to cause mayhem in many parts of the world. The review conference adopted an outcome document with four sections including an implementation plan for the period of 2012 to 2018.[64] Implementation of this program can substantially contribute not only to the advancement of this issue but also to the advancement of international peace and security at large.[65]

Conclusion

Toward a Culture of Peace

During my term as president of the General Assembly, we marked the thirteenth anniversary of a momentous action by consensus, taken on September 13, 1999, to adopt the United Nations Declaration and Programme of Action on the Culture of Peace. With this landmark adoption, the General Assembly laid down a charter for the new millennium. This historic, norm-setting document is rightly considered one of the most significant and enduring legacies of the United Nations.[1]

The culture of peace is a set of values, attitudes, and ways of life based on the principles of freedom, justice, democracy, tolerance, solidarity, and respect for diversity, as well as on dialogue and understanding. Through the efforts of the United Nations, civil society, regional organizations, and peace-loving states, a global movement for the culture of peace is emerging.

The Declaration identifies eight specific areas of action to be taken at all levels—by the individual, the family, the community, the nation, the region, and the globe. As I took office on the International Day of Peace in 2011, I stated my personal commitment to "emphasize the need for the full and effective implementation of Declaration and Programme of Action on a Culture of Peace, in cooperation, of course, with governments, the Secretary-General and civil society."[2]

On September 14, 2012, we held a High-Level Forum on the Culture of Peace at which we renewed this commitment. In my remarks, I highlighted three crucial dimensions of the Declaration and Programme of

Action. First, the Declaration takes a comprehensive approach covering eight specific areas of action—from education to understanding, tolerance, and solidarity to international peace and security. Second, it pays special attention to the individual's self-transformation. Targeting the individual is meaningful because there cannot be true peace unless the individual mind is at peace. Third, the Declaration and Programme of Action galvanizes a wide array of actors, from parents to teachers, professionals to religious leaders, artists to intellectuals, truly engaging society as a whole.

In addition, civil society and the media have been given a very prominent role in promoting the culture of peace. Indeed, the first of the eight action areas describes how to foster the culture of peace through education. I strongly believe that if the culture of peace is to take deeper root in us and among us, then we will need to reach out more effectively to younger minds as they develop. We must place crucial focus on peace education. Today's youth deserve a radically different education—one that does not glorify war but educates for peace, nonviolence, and global understanding.

We should also be aware that nonviolence can only truly flourish when the world is freed from poverty, hunger, and discrimination—and when women and men can realize their highest potential and live a secure and fulfilling life. Inequality, injustice, and exclusion generate structural violence that is incompatible with peace at both national and international levels. Another area we need to concentrate on is giving long-overdue recognition to the fact that women have a major role to play in promoting the culture of peace and in bringing about lasting peace and reconciliation, particularly in strife-torn societies. Unless women are at the forefront of the promotion and practice of the culture of peace, long-term solutions will elude us.

The cause of peace needs to be understood not only in the passive sense of the absence of war but also in the constructive sense of creating conditions for equality and social justice. As Martin Luther King Jr. affirmed, "We must concentrate not merely on the negative expulsion of war but the positive affirmation of peace."[3] In short, the human right to peace needs to be established as an autonomous right by the international community.

Furthermore, every one of us must be a true believer in peace and nonviolence and practice what we profess. Whether at the UN, at intergovernmental conferences, in places of worship, in schools, or in our homes, a lot can be achieved in promoting the culture of peace through individual resolve and action. The work of promoting the culture of peace is a continuous process. Each of us can make a difference in that process.[4]

A diplomat's constant effort, often behind the public glare, is to search for peace where there is war, to find solid bases for consensus, for mediation, and even better, for the prevention of conflicts. But diplomats do not deal solely with dangerous differences between states. They spend much of their time, at least at the United Nations, trying, in coordination with civil society and NGOs, to help the disenfranchised, to address forgotten issues.

As you have read, during my presidency of the General Assembly, we fostered programs to raise awareness of the terrible scourge of violence against women. We sought to ensure that the mentally disabled are not left out of global health plans and that noncommunicable diseases such as obesity and diabetes receive proper recognition as growing epidemics. We made certain that the most vulnerable—the millions of refugees and internally displaced persons that shame our civilization—receive our support. This work is not done only in grand conference halls and official meetings.

During my tenure as president, I have personally witnessed the price of our failures in the streets of Mogadishu and in the Dadaab camp in Kenya, where over half a million people struggle, every day, to survive. I also went to Libya to represent the world community just after the fall of Gaddafi and witnessed firsthand the devastation left behind by an ugly dictatorship. These journeys provide essential legitimacy for diplomatic initiatives.

On September 12, 2012, I was awarded an honorary doctor of laws degree by Fordham University. As I said on that occasion, universities provide the necessary ambience and resources for the study and analysis of past experiences in order to design better plans and practical guidance for future efforts. Universities offer an ideal place for gaining perspective, for sharing wisdom, for understanding, and for encouraging dialogue. These are essential building blocks as we strive to strengthen those "bridges to peace" that are at times elusive. This is the common ground that diplomats require to craft workable treaties, conventions, and laws.

I welcome the opportunity to engage with students. As PGA, my office sponsored fifteen student internships over the course of one year. As permanent representative of Qatar, I previously sponsored at least thirty more, and I continue welcoming new interns in my current capacity as high representative to the Alliance of Civilizations. I assign advisers to answer the interns' questions and involve them in the drafting of speeches and organizing of meetings.

Throughout my diplomatic career, my overriding goal has been to equip people—whether students, scholars, or diplomats—with the tools and knowledge to overcome cultural barriers. Person by person, let us strive for a civilization that unites rather than divides, one that can truly celebrate the diversity of the human race as we continue the endless struggle for a more equitable world where justice and peace might reign.[5]

In Closing

In closing, I would like to highlight what I believe to be the main achievements of the 66th session. To start with, there is no doubt that we are living through an extraordinary moment in the history of the Middle East and North Africa. Our attention in the region now extends beyond the Arab-Israeli conflict to developments concerning the Arab Awakening and how to support the legitimate aspirations of the citizens of many of these countries for democratic change.

Today, the legitimate demands of the peoples of the region for liberty, dignity, and social justice continue to ring out loudly across the region. Recognizing that these demands are consistent with the basic principles and objectives of the UN Charter, as well as with international human rights standards, the UN has been—and will remain—at the forefront of international efforts to defend our shared values and to support these legitimate changes, while respecting each country's sovereignty and territorial integrity.

On the issue of Palestine, we witnessed a historic development when the president of the Palestinian Authority, Mr. Mahmoud Abbas, transmitted Palestine's application for membership to the United Nations to the secretary-general on September 23, 2012. I had the honor to process, along with the secretary-general, Palestine's first request to join the membership. Although it was not possible to welcome Palestine as a new member during my mandate, I was very encouraged by the elevation of Palestine to nonmember observer-state status on November 29, 2012. It is my conviction that the General Assembly should continue to work collectively for the attainment of a just and comprehensive peace in the Middle East.

On Libya, the General Assembly made the historic decision to affirm the rights of the new Libyan authorities, both in the General Assembly and the Human Rights Council. The Assembly thereby played a key role in the admission and adoption of the credentials of the true representatives of the Libyan people. In November 2011, I made a joint visit to Libya with the secretary-general to demonstrate that the United Nations supported the Libyans as they embarked on this critical journey of reconciliation, reconstruction, and democracy.

On Syria, the General Assembly frequently expressed its concern regarding the ongoing crisis, in keeping with its institutional responsibility related to international peace and security when there is deadlock in the Security Council. In December 2011, the General Assembly adopted a resolution condemning the continued grave and systematic human rights violations committed by the Syrian authorities. In February 2012, the General Assembly adopted resolution 66/253, which led to the appointment of the joint special envoy of the United Nations and the League of Arab States.

In August 2012, the Assembly convened another timely meeting on Syria where member states adopted another resolution aimed at bringing the crisis to an end. I also organized several formal and informal meetings of the General Assembly, in order for member states to be kept informed, to hear the views of the main UN actors, and to express their national positions. I believe the General Assembly has a crucial role to play in ensuring that the violence in Syria ends quickly.

Key advancements were also made in each of the four areas I identified as a pillar of my presidency. On the first pillar, "the peaceful settlement of disputes," the Assembly has provided space for extensive deliberations and increased the momentum around mediation. Beginning with the General Debate on this topic in September 2011, many meetings, conferences, and seminars were subsequently held throughout the year, both at the UN and beyond New York. These discussions led to the informal high-level meeting of the General Assembly in May.

I am pleased to see that concrete deliberations and actions have already taken place to materialize the ideas emerging from these discussions. The adoption of the follow-up resolution on mediation on September 13, 2012, reflects the eagerness of the membership to actively pursue this issue.[6]

I have always believed that dialogue among civilizations offers a complementary approach to preventing and peacefully resolving conflicts, and I have placed a special focus on the United Nations Alliance of Civilizations. Its role could be critical, particularly in addressing disputes emanating from cultural or religious differences. I see more room in this respect for further elaboration. The Alliance should also be strengthened so that it can fulfill its noble mission more effectively.

As UN high representative for the Alliance of Civilizations and beyond, I will continue to invest my time and efforts in supporting this vision.

I deplore and condemn any acts that amount to the defamation of religions and incitement to hatred and xenophobia, and I strongly condemned the attacks against consulates and embassies, especially where diplomatic personnel and ordinary citizens have been killed or injured. Violence is never the answer. I implore citizens of the world to open their hearts and their minds, to celebrate the common values that bind us all in this one human family. Inspired by the spirited enthusiasm of the General Assembly's High-Level Forum on the Culture of Peace on September 14, 2012, I proposed that this should become an annual event, to be held every year on the anniversary of the adoption the Declaration and Programme of Action by consensus in 1999.

The second pillar I identified was "UN reform and revitalization." Recognizing that the United Nations must adapt to the global realities of the twenty-first century in order to fulfill its mandate, I worked throughout the year to support the endeavors of the two cofacilitators on General Assembly revitalization, with the aim of fostering consensus among the general membership. The Ad Hoc Working Group on Assembly revitalization also held many important discussions, from which emerged a broad consensus on the importance of Assembly revitalization and the urgent need for a truly viable Assembly.

Throughout the session, I stressed the pressing need for a balanced approach in considering this issue, taking into account both the implementation of Assembly resolutions and other administrative initiatives aimed at enhancing its efficiency. I would also note the increasingly active role of the president of the General Assembly and his office, as noted in the recently adopted resolution on Assembly revitalization and the request of member states that the secretary-general should submit (in the context of the proposed program budget for the biennium 2014–2015) proposals to review the budget allocation to the Office of the President of the General Assembly. This is most welcome.

On Security Council reform, I was very much aware of the need to strengthen confidence in this process, so I immediately reappointed Ambassador Zahir Tanin to chair the intergovernmental negotiations. I am pleased that, under my presidency, the eighth round of the intergovernmental negotiations took place. Many member states acknowledged a new momentum and an increased level of candor, interaction, and engagement in this round. Now it is for the member states to continue to build on the achievements to date and to act to crystallize the areas of convergence.

The third pillar I identified this session was "improving disaster prevention and response." At the beginning of the session, I expressed serious concern about the humanitarian crisis in the Horn of Africa. In December 2011, I undertook a joint official visit to Somalia together with the secretary-general. We both felt that it was very important to visit the country to demonstrate that the United Nations and its member states continue to stand with the Somalis on their path to a better future. As president of the General Assembly, I extended to the government and the people of Somalia my commitment to help ensure a better, safer, and more prosperous tomorrow.

In April 2012, we held the General Assembly's Informal Thematic Debate on Disaster Risk Reduction. It was clear during this event that there is unprecedented international momentum to reduce disaster risk. Participants emphasized the importance of integrating disaster risk reduction with any future framework on sustainable development. I am pleased that the results of the thematic debate have been useful for member states in drafting the Rio+20 outcome document.

We also heard that addressing disaster risk requires the multifaceted engagement of all stakeholders, including the private sector and civil society. The integration of humanitarian and development approaches to strengthen local resilience and to mitigate the risk of disasters is also an essential part of an overall disaster reduction framework. Overall, it was clear that the international community needs to be better equipped to respond to disasters, both natural and man-made. I would like to note here the relevance of the resolution on improving the effectiveness and coordination of military and civil defense assets for natural disaster response (HOPEFOR), and I would encourage member states to build on this concept.

My fourth pillar was "sustainable development and global prosperity." The 66th session was, of course, a landmark year for sustainable development. The United Nations Conference on Sustainable Development (Rio+20) will go down in history as the moment when the international community renewed its political will and commitment to tackling the interconnected economic, social, and environmental challenges we face.

The implementation of the Rio+20 outcome document will require the highest level of political commitment, and I would stress the importance of putting in place the effective means of implementation, transfer of technology, and inclusion of the whole range of partners—civil society and the private sector—in this process.

A defining element of Rio+20 was also that it launched an intergovernmental process to define Sustainable Development Goals (SDGs) after 2015. The role of the General Assembly is central in this exercise. As requested in the Rio outcome document, I appointed Ambassador Maria Luiza Ribeiro Viotti of Brazil to establish an open working group with a view to developing the SDGs. I once again express my hope that the member states will exercise flexibility and a spirit of compromise in this process.

In the field of global economics, our main focus has been to help strengthen the governance of the world economy. The empowerment of the General Assembly in economic matters was sought not for its own sake but because we deeply believe that the Assembly has a central role to play in global governance. Forging legitimate political consensus is what the General Assembly does best, and that is precisely what is needed today in global governance. At the High-Level Thematic Debate on the State of the World Economy, world leaders stressed that without our collective response and strong leadership, the world economy will continue to face serious challenges.

Throughout my term, I reminded the global community that if we are to rethink the way we do development, it is also important to rethink and reshape some of our organizations and intergovernmental bodies. I coorganized a three-part seminar series on the Quadrennial Comprehensive Policy Review (QCPR) of operational activities for development of the UN system. The QCPR is a timely exercise, offering a forward-looking reflection on the longer-term strategic repositioning of the UN development system within the development landscape. I would emphasize the importance of the QCPR resolution, which directly impacts the day-to-day work of the UN system and will shape the strategic plans of the more than thirty entities that compose the UN development system.[7]

In addition to my four pillars, the Assembly of course tackled many other important topics. I would like to highlight here just a few more achievements of the Assembly. Disarmament and international security remained high on the General Assembly's agenda throughout the 66th session. During my discussions with member states, I called on all to maintain a constructive and forward-looking approach and to aim at consensus building to the maximum extent possible.

I also expressed my concern about the current status of the disarmament machinery, including during my visit to address the Conference on Disarmament in Geneva. Although member states advanced their work throughout the session on almost the entire scope of issues on the agenda of the First Committee, greater efforts and flexibility from all involved are needed to advance the multilateral disarmament negotiations.

In the run-up to the 2015 Review Conference of the Treaty on the Non-Proliferation of Nuclear Weapons, the implementation of disarmament and nonproliferation commitments, in accordance with the treaty and in line with the plans of action adopted in 2010, will be crucial for the success of that conference. In this context, equally important will be the realization of real progress at the Middle East Conference on the Establishment of a Zone Free from Nuclear Weapons and Other

Weapons of Mass Destruction. I am aware that some serious groundwork has been done and look forward to the conference convening successfully with the participation of all states of the region.

On peacekeeping, during my intensive exchanges with member states, I expressed my gratitude to them for their dedication and perseverance in ensuring that our organization succeeds in fulfilling its mandate. The importance that all member states attach to issues related to peacekeeping cannot be underscored enough. This is because decisions on financing, on elaborating policies and guidelines, and on reviewing implementation pertain to the authority of the General Assembly and its 193 member states. This has been, and will be, essential to strengthening the legitimacy of the actions of the General Assembly.

The safety and security of our peacekeepers has been on the Assembly's agenda on various occasions. The General Assembly and its member states have to continue working closely with host countries, which bear the primary responsibility for safety and security of peacekeeping personnel in their respective territories. I have also stressed the importance of a strengthened global partnership among all stakeholders in peacekeeping operations, in particular, host countries, troop contributors, regional organizations, and UN staff. Member states must continue to build this partnership and maximize the use of national capacities while providing rapid and effective international assistance.

The intergovernmental process on the reform of the human rights treaty bodies has advanced this session, as well. The independence of treaty bodies in the protection and promotion of human rights should remain the cornerstone of this reform process.

On September 24, 2012, the General Assembly held its first-ever High-Level Meeting on the Rule of Law. This meeting has generated great interest from member states and civil society, indicating its importance in our societies and in international affairs. Preparations for the substantive outcome document and other necessary arrangements have been a priority during the 66th session to ensure a productive and successful high-level meeting in the 67th session.

Under my presidency, the General Assembly held a Thematic Debate on Drugs and Crime as a Threat to Development in June 2012. The summary of the proceedings was transmitted to the Thirteenth UN Congress on Crime Prevention and Criminal Justice scheduled to take place in Doha, Qatar, in 2015.

The Third Counter-Terrorism plenary review in June resulted in the adoption of a consensual resolution. The counterterrorism seminar that I organized just before the plenary was a useful occasion for various stakeholders to interact on this major issue that affects us all.

On health issues, in September 2011, we had the first-ever General Assembly High-Level Meeting on the Prevention and Control of Noncommunicable Diseases (NCDs). This was a landmark meeting, where NCDs were given well-deserved priority on the global development agenda. A mandate was established, and clear responsibilities were delineated. Work on implementation began in 2012, and throughout the session, I encouraged member states to consider broadening the definition of NCDs to include mental health disorders.

On the crucial issue of the budget, the Assembly adopted by consensus the program budget for biennium 2012–2013 in an amount of US$5.152 billion. It also approved by consensus the financing of the UN's sixteen peacekeeping missions in the amount of US$7.234 billion. A number of important resolutions were adopted without a vote on critical issues relating to policy, administrative, and financial matters for the effective functioning of the UN.

As the president, I convened a brainstorming meeting of the Fifth Committee, followed by a retreat, to initiate an informal discussion on the longstanding need for the review of the Fifth Committee's internal working methods. Here, there was much convergence in the views of the member states, and the two events that I convened contributed positively to strengthening the relationship of mutual trust and good faith among all stakeholders. I believe that such discussions, in both informal and formal settings, should be sustained in coming sessions, not only as a stock-taking but also as important trust-building exercises, with a view to rationalizing and optimizing the deliberations of the Fifth Committee and bringing greater efficiency to the work of the Assembly. I wish the 67th session great success in considering the scale of assessment.

A word on our partners: at the outset of the session, I affirmed my commitment to building a truly united global partnership both inside and outside the United Nations. I believe strongly that civil society has an important role to play in achieving inclusive and sustainable development, peace and security, and human rights, as well as in ensuring public support for the UN's agenda. I was very pleased to interact with many NGO representatives in most all of our themes and debates. Representatives of civil society and the NGO community were highly instrumental in the success of the brilliant event we held in February 2012 to mark World Inter-Faith Harmony Week, attended by twelve hundred people of various religions. I would note, however, that the capacity of the Office of the President to reach out to civil society should be strengthened to ensure continuity and an adequate level of support to this increasingly important function.

September 17, 2012, marked the closing of the 66th session of the General Assembly and the end of my term as its president. It had been a remarkable and momentous session. The events of the year 2011–2012 formed a moment in history that will remain in our minds for decades to come. It was a year when the impact of the global financial and economic crisis put the international community to a challenging test. But it was also a year of renewed hope as countries emerged from conflict to peace, as populations across the world continued to call for freedom, dignity, and justice.

Of course, as PGA, I faced my share of difficult situations "behind the scenes." On one occasion, a UN representative tried to use legal procedure to block the human rights commissioner from addressing the Assembly about possible abuses in his country. I denied his request, offering only to bring it to a vote, which he declined. On other occasions, I had to reject draft resolutions that I knew would be defeated, rather than bring them to a failed vote that would reflect negatively on the organization. A different sort of political challenge was posed by the death of a head of state reviled by some nations. I was fortunate to have had thirteen years of experience representing my country and enjoyed excellent relationships with member states, relationships that helped me navigate these and other challenges.

Looking back at the difficulties and opportunities we encountered during the 66th session, I am proud to say that the General Assembly stood strong, active, and responsive. New partnerships were formed, political commitments were renewed, and results-oriented actions were taken. I feel that I served in a fair and transparent manner, representing the interests of all member states. Building on our mutual understanding, I personally introduced two resolutions, the first establishing Global Parents Day and the second establishing International Happiness Day.[8] I frequently held bilateral meetings with the P5 and others. It would have been helpful to have more time (two or three years, ideally) to accomplish everything I set out to do as PGA. However, I made the most of the time I was given. My efforts outside the UN demanded no less than fifty overseas trips including to the European Parliament, which I was the first president of the General Assembly to address. If I had the chance to do it again, there is nothing I would change.

I believe I succeeded in making the General Assembly and the office of the president more visible internationally. Whether this enhanced visibility will persist is in large part up to the presidents who succeed me. Some presidents of the General Assembly are very active and take initiative; others have little experience at the UN and spend the first six months of their terms learning the system. I hope my actions will influence future leaders of the General Assembly.

Whatever the future holds, it is a source of profound honor and pride to have led the UN membership during a critical moment in history. It was a privilege to work with the 193 member states, and I am most grateful for their cooperation and support and their enduring commitment to the mission of the United Nations.

I would like to note, in particular, the strong working relationship and great friendship that I enjoyed with the secretary-general, His Excellency Mr. Ban Ki-moon. Determined to enhance the coherence of the UN's efforts, the secretary-general and I worked in close partnership throughout the year. It has been my deep pleasure to work with Mr. Ban, who is a true leader—dedicated, genuine, and relentless in his pursuit of a better world.

Our work during the 66th session of the General Assembly would not have been possible without the full and remarkable support of the State of Qatar. I wish to express my very special gratitude and appreciation to His Highness Sheikh Hamad bin Khalifa Al-Thani, the emir of the State of Qatar; and to His Highness Sheikh Tamim Bin Hamad Al-Thani, the heir apparent of the State of Qatar; as well as to His Excellency, Sheikh Hamad bin Jassim bin Jabr Al-Thani, the prime minister and minister for foreign affairs of the State of Qatar; and also to His Excellency, Dr. Khalid Bin Mohammad Al Attiyah, minister of State for foreign affairs of Qatar. Their immense support and commitment to the United Nations have helped us greatly in serving the United Nations and the world.

I promised the member states a successful session at the beginning of my mandate. With an outstanding team in my cabinet, representing the diversity of the General Assembly, we worked very hard, and I believe we met expectations. I wish to acknowledge, for the record, the invaluable support of this outstanding team and the tremendous roles played by two of Qatar's most talented diplomats, namely, my chief of Cabinet, His Excellency Ambassador Mutlaq Al-Qahtani, and my deputy chief of cabinet, Ambassador Tariq Al-Ansari. You are indeed great assets for your country and for this organization.

I would also like to express my deep gratitude to the highly professional UN colleagues who worked diligently, day in and day out, to make the 66th session run smoothly and successfully. In particular, I thank the staff of the Department of General Assembly Affairs and Conference Management, who earned my enduring appreciation. My special thanks to the interpreters, security personnel, and protocol staff for all their hard work. I am also especially grateful to staff of the Department of Public Information for their valuable support. To every single person who helped and supported the 66th session: thank you.

To the distinguished delegates and representatives of member states: we worked as a team. You guided and supported me very much, and I applaud you for all that we achieved together during the 66th session.

On a more personal note, I would like to acknowledge my gratitude to my family for joining me on this journey. My son, Aziz, was only six years old the year I served as PGA. The demands of my schedule meant that although we lived in the same house, I would sometimes not see him for days—leaving before he was awake in the morning and returning after had gone to sleep at night. On the other hand, he often visited me in my office after school and liked to tell his classmates that his father was "the president." I was also able to take him with me on several trips including to meet the pope. So, as much as it was a sacrifice, the experiences Aziz had with me that year will certainly enrich his education and, hopefully, his life. Finally, I am so very grateful to my lovely wife, Muna, for her support that year and always. I am especially glad I was able to use the opportunity of my election as PGA to benefit the UN Trust Fund to End Violence Against Women, for which she advocates as chair of UN Women for Peace. The event, featuring the Qatar Philharmonic orchestra, drew thirteen hundred people and raised a good amount of money for this worthwhile cause.

In conclusion, as I look forward, I see the need for a universal and truly legitimate United Nations growing ever more paramount. No organization in the world maintains as all encompassing a global mandate as the UN does. And no organization has the potential—and the responsibility—to build peace and prosperity for all the way the UN does.

I am very confident that the United Nations will continue to offer humankind the best platform for a world of peace, security, and prosperity for all. I look forward to continuing in my diplomatic efforts to realize this vision for the future.

NOTES

NOTES TO THE PREFACE

1. Nassir Abdulaziz Al-Nasser, "On the Occasion of a Dialogue with Civil Society" (New York, NY, October 4, 2011), http://www.un.org/en/ga/president/66/statements/civilsociety041011.html.
2. Nassir Abdulaziz Al-Nasser, "Opening Remarks of the President of the 66th Session of the United Nations General Assembly" (New York, NY, September 13, 2011), http://www.un.org/en/ga/president/66/statements/openingremarks-13092011.shtml.
3. Han Seung-soo, *Beyond the Shadow of 9/11: A Year at the United Nations General Assembly* (Washington, DC: Edwin O. Reischauer Center for East Asian Studies, Johns Hopkins University–SAIS, 2007), 100.
4. Nassir Abdulaziz Al-Nasser, "Remarks at the Election of the President of the 67th Session of the General Assembly" (New York, NY, June 8, 2012), http://www.un.org/en/ga/president/66/statements/pga67election080612.shtml.

NOTES TO CHAPTER 1

1. Immanuel Kant, *Perpetual Peace* (Minneapolis: Filiquarian, 2007).
2. Charter of the United Nations, http://www.un.org/en/documents/charter/.
3. Nassir Abdulaziz Al-Nasser, "The United Nations and the Business of Universality" (New York University, New York, NY, February 13, 2012), http://www.un.org/en/ga/president/66/statements/nyu130212.shtml. For the Universal Declaration of Human Rights, see http://www.un.org/en/documents/udhr/.
4. United Nations General Assembly Resolution 55.2, "United Nations Millennium Declaration," September 18, 2000, http://www.un.org/millennium/declaration/ares552e.pdf.
5. Nassir Abdulaziz Al-Nasser, "How Relevant Is the UN to the Solutions of Today's World Problems?" (Institute of Oriental Studies of the Russian Academy of Sciences, Moscow, Russia, May 2, 2012), http://www.un.org/en/ga/president/66/statements/moscowlecture020512.shtml.
6. United Nations, "Millennium Development Goals—Background," http://www.un.org/millenniumgoals/bkgd.shtml.

7. Nassir Abdulaziz Al-Nasser, "Global Challenges and the Role of the UN at the Dawn of the 21st Century" (Oxford Centre for Islamic Studies, Oxford, UK, March 1, 2012), http://www.un.org/en/ga/president/66/statements/oxford010312.shtml.

8. United Nations, "Background Information on the Responsibility to Protect," http://www.un.org/en/preventgenocide/rwanda/about/bgresponsibility.shtml.

9. Kofi Annan, "We the Peoples," report of the secretary-general, Millennium Summit (United Nations, New York, NY, September 2000), 5.

10. International Commission on Intervention and State Sovereignty, *The Responsibility to Protect: Report of the International Commission on Intervention and State Sovereignty* (Ottawa, ON: International Development Research Centre, December 2001), http://responsibilitytoprotect.org/ICISS%20Report.pdf.

11. Kofi Annan, "Follow-Up to the Outcome of the Millennium Summit," note by the secretary-general (United Nations, New York, NY, December 2, 2004), 57, http://daccess-ods.un.org/access.nsf/Get?Open&DS=A/59/565&Lang=E.

12. Kofi Annan, "In Larger Freedom: Towards Development, Security, and Human Rights for All," report of the secretary-general (United Nations, New York, NY, March 21, 2005), 35, http://www.un.org/Docs/journal/asp/ws.asp?m=A/59/2005.

13. United Nations General Assembly Resolution 60.1, "2005 World Summit Outcome" (paras. 138–140), http://www.un.org/en/ga/search/view_doc.asp?symbol=A/RES/60/1.

14. Al-Nasser, "The United Nations and the Business of Universality."

15. Nassir Abdulaziz Al-Nasser, "Reflections on the Value of the UN's Role in the World" (Cathedral of Saint John the Divine, New York, NY, September 25, 2011), http://www.un.org/en/ga/president/66/statements/cathedralchurch250911.html.

16. Al-Nasser, "Global Challenges."

17. Al-Nasser, "The United Nations and the Business of Universality."

18. Han Seung-soo, *Beyond the Shadow of 9/11: A Year at the United Nations General Assembly* (Washington DC: Edwin O. Reischauer Center for East Asian Studies, Johns Hopkins University–SAIS, 2007), 25.

19. Nassir Abdulaziz Al-Nasser, "On the Occasion of the Opening of the General Debate" (United Nations, New York, NY, September 21, 2011), http://www.un.org/en/ga/president/66/statements/generaldebate21092011.shtml.

20. Nassir Abdulaziz Al-Nasser, "The United Nations, the Road to Civilization and Development" (Moroccan Academy for Diplomatic Studies, Rabat, Morocco, July 5, 2012), http://www.un.org/en/ga/president/66/statements/MoroccanAcademy 050712%20.shtml.

21. United Nations General Assembly Resolution 65/283, "Strengthening the Role of Mediation in the Peaceful Settlement of Disputes, Conflict Prevention and Resolution," July 28, 2011, http://www.un.org/ga/search/view_doc.asp?symbol=A/RES/65/283.

22. Al-Nasser, "On the Occasion of the Opening of the General Debate."

23. Nassir Abdulaziz Al-Nasser, "Opening Remarks of the President of the 66th

Session of the United Nations General Assembly" (New York, NY, September 13, 2011), http://www.un.org/en/ga/president/66/statements/openingremarks -13092011.shtml.

24. Nassir Abdulaziz Al-Nasser, "On the Occasion of the Closing of the General Debate" (United Nations, New York, NY, September 27, 2011), http://www.un.org/ en/ga/president/66/statements/gdclosing270911.shtml.

25. Al-Nasser, "Opening Remarks of the President"

26. For the procedure by which the Charter may be amended, see Charter of the United Nations, chapter 18, articles 108–109, http://www.un.org/en/documents/ charter/chapter18.shtml.

27. International Monetary Fund, "Factsheet—How the IMF Makes Decisions." September 10, 20013, http://www.imf.org/external/np/exr/facts/govern.htm.

28. Al-Nasser, "Global Challenges."

29. Al-Nasser, "On the Occasion of the Closing of the General Debate."

30. Al-Nasser, "Opening Remarks of the President."

31. Al-Nasser, "Global Challenges."

32. Nassir Abdulaziz Al-Nasser, "Remarks at the Special High-Level Meeting of ECO-SOC with the Bretton Woods Institutions, the World Trade Organization, and the United Nations Conference on Trade and Development" (New York, NY, March 12, 2012), http://www.un.org/en/ga/president/66/statements/ecosoc120312.shtml.

33. Nassir Abdulaziz Al-Nasser, "On the Occasion of the G-77 and China Ministerial Meeting" (New York, NY, September 23, 2011), http://www.un.org/en/ga/ president/66/statements/g77mtg230911.shtml.

34. Al-Nasser, "Opening Remarks of the President."

35. Al-Nasser, "The United Nations, the Road to Civilization and Development."

36. Al-Nasser, "On the Occasion of the Closing of the General Debate."

37. United Nations Security Council Department of Public Information, "Security Council Requests African Union to Increase Troop Level of Somalia Mission" (New York, NY, February 22, 2012), https://www.un.org/News/Press/docs//2012/ sc10550.doc.htm.

38. Al-Nasser, "Opening Remarks of the President."

39. United Nations General Assembly Resolution 66/288, "The Future We Want," September 11, 2012, http://www.un.org/en/ga/search/view_doc.asp?symbol=%20A/ RES/66/288.

40. Al-Nasser, "The United Nations, the Road to Civilization and Development."

41. Al-Nasser, "Opening Remarks of the President."

42. Al-Nasser, "On the Occasion of the Opening of the General Debate."

43. Al-Nasser, "On the Occasion of the Closing of the General Debate."

44. United Nations General Assembly Resolution 67/19, "Status of Palestine in the United Nations," December 4, 2012, http://www.un.org/ga/search/view_doc.asp? symbol=A/RES/67/19.

45. Al-Nasser, "The United Nations, the Road to Civilization and Development."

46. "South-South Cooperation," *Wikipedia*, http://en.wikipedia.org/wiki/South%
E2%80%93South_cooperation. See also Guido Ashoff, World Bank Institute,
"Triangular Cooperation: Opportunities, Risks, and Conditions for Effectiveness," October 2010, http://wbi.worldbank.org/wbi/devoutreach/article/531/
triangular-cooperation-opportunties-risks-and-conditions-effectiveness.
47. Al-Nasser, "On the Occasion of the G-77 and China Ministerial Meeting."
48. Nassir Abdulaziz Al-Nasser, "On the Occasion of a Dialogue with Civil Society" (New York, NY, October 4, 2011), http://www.un.org/en/ga/president/66/
statements/civilsociety041011.html.
49. Al-Nasser, "On the Occasion of the Closing of the General Debate."
50. Francis Fukuyama, *The End of History and the Last Man* (New York: Free Press,
1992).
51. Nassir Abdulaziz Al-Nasser, "How Universal Are Universal Values?" (Bait el
Hikma, Carthage, Tunisia, June 13, 2012), http://www.un.org/en/ga/president/66/
statements/tunisia130612.shtml.
52. Mustapha Tlili, "Europe and Islam: Shared History, Shared Identity, Shared Destiny," in *Can There Be Life without the Other? The Possibilities and Limits of Inter-
culturality*, Gulbenkian Conference Report, 177–187 (Lisbon, Portugal: Fundação
Calouste Gulbenkian, 2009).
53. Al-Nasser, "Global Challenges"; Maria Rosa Menocal, *The Ornament of the World*
(New York: Little, Brown, 2002).
54. Nassir Abdulaziz Al-Nasser, "Challenges of the Transition in the Arab Region:
Economic and Social Policies in the Region" (Cairo, Egypt, October 12, 2011),
http://www.un.org/en/ga/president/66/statements/arabregion121011.shtml.
55. Al-Nasser, "The United Nations and the Business of Universality."
56. Al-Nasser, "How Universal Are Universal Values?"
57. United Nations Development Programme, "Reports 1990–2013: The Human
Development Report," http://hdr.undp.org/en/reports/about/.
58. Nassir Abdulaziz Al-Nasser, "The Middle East and North Africa at the Dawn of
the 21st Century: Challenges and Hopes" (Moscow State University, May 3, 2012),
http://www.un.org/en/ga/president/66/statements/middleeast_northafrica_hopes
030512.shtml.
59. Al-Nasser, "Challenges of the Transition in the Arab Region."
60. Al-Nasser, "How Universal Are Universal Values?"
61. Charter of the United Nations, Preamble, http://www.un.org/en/documents/
charter/preamble.shtml.
62. United Nations General Assembly Committee on Information, http://www.un.org/
en/ga/coi/.
63. International Telecommunication Union, "Overview," http://www.itu.int/en/about/
Pages/default.aspx.
64. UN Office for Outer Space Affairs, "United Nations Committee on the Peaceful
Uses of Outer Space," http://www.oosa.unvienna.org/oosa/COPUOS/copuos.html.

65. Al-Nasser, "Global Challenges."

66. Nassir Abdulaziz Al-Nasser, "Remarks on the Occasion of the Special Cultural Event Celebrating the 66th Session of the General Assembly and Supporting UN Women" (New York, NY, June 6, 2012), http://www.un.org/en/ga/president/66/statements/66-6-6concerto60612.shtml.

67. General Assembly of the United Nations, Credentials Committee, http://www.un.org/en/ga/credentials/credentials.shtml.

68. United Nations General Assembly 66/176, "Situation of Human Rights in the Syrian Arab Republic," December 19, 2011, http://www.un.org/en/ga/search/view_doc.asp?symbol=%20A/RES/66/176.

69. Brendan O'Leary, "United Nations Mediation: Experiences and Reflections from the Field," summary report (New York, NY, November 23, 2011), http://www.un.org/en/ga/president/66/Letters/PDF/Mediation%20Summary%20-%2023%20November%202011.pdf.

70. United Nations Alliance of Civilizations, "Doha," http://www.unaoc.org/events/global-forums/doha/. The report of the forum is available at http://unaoc.org/docs/UANOC%20Doha%20Forum%20Report.pdf.

71. United Nations General Assembly Resolution 53/243, "Declaration and Programme of Action on a Culture of Peace," October 6, 1999, http://daccess-dds-ny.un.org/doc/UNDOC/GEN/N99/774/43/PDF/N9977443.pdf?OpenElement.

72. United Nations General Assembly Resolution 66/10, "United Nations Counter-Terrorism Centre," December 7, 2011, http://www.un.org/ga/search/view_doc.asp?symbol=%20A/RES/66/10.

73. Nassir Abdulaziz Al-Nasser, "Remarks on the Occasion of the Closing of the Main Part of the Session" (United Nations, New York, NY, December 23, 2011), http://www.un.org/en/ga/president/66/statements/closingsession231211.shtml.

74. Niccolò Machiavelli, The Prince, trans. William J. Connell (New York: Bedford / St. Martin's, 2005).

75. Al-Nasser, "Global Challenges."

76. Al-Nasser, "Remarks on the Occasion of the Special Cultural Event."

77. Nassir Abdulaziz Al-Nasser, "Remarks at the Argentine Foreign Service Academy" (Buenos Aires, Argentina, June 25, 2012), http://www.un.org/en/ga/president/66/statements/ArgentineForeignAcademy250612.shtml.

78. Al-Nasser, "The United Nations and the Business of Universality."

79. Al-Nasser, "On the Occasion of the G-77 and China Ministerial Meeting."

80. Al-Nasser, "The United Nations and the Business of Universality."

NOTES TO CHAPTER 2

1. Nassir Abdulaziz Al-Nasser, "Opening Remarks at the High Level Meeting of the General Assembly on the Role of the Member States in Mediation" (New York, NY, May 23, 2012), http://www.un.org/en/ga/president/66/statements/mediation230512.shtml.

2. United Nations General Assembly Resolution 65/283, "Strengthening the Role of Mediation in the Peaceful Settlement of Disputes, Conflict Prevention and Resolution," July 28, 2011, http://www.un.org/ga/search/view_doc.asp?symbol=A/RES/65/283.

3. Nassir Abdulaziz Al-Nasser, "On the Occasion of the International Istanbul Conference on 'Enhancing Peace through Mediation': New Actors, Fresh Approaches, Bold Initiatives" (Istanbul, Turkey, February 25, 2012), http://www.un.org/en/ga/president/66/statements/istanbul250212.shtml.

4. Han Seung-soo, *Beyond the Shadow of 9/11: A Year at the United Nations General Assembly* (Washington, DC: Edwin O. Reischauer Center for East Asian Studies, Johns Hopkins University–SAIS, 2007), 43.

5. Nassir Abdulaziz Al-Nasser, "On the Occasion of the Breakfast Meeting of the Group of Friends of Mediation" (New York, NY, September 20, 2011), http://www.un.org/en/ga/president/66/statements/mediation20092011.shtml.

6. United Nations Security Council, "Statement by the President of the Security Council," report (New York, NY, September 23, 2010), http://www.securitycouncilreport.org/atf/cf/%7B65BFCF9B-6D27-4E9C-8CD3-CF6E4FF96FF9%7D/PBC%20S%20PRST%202010%2018.pdf. See also United Nations, "Security Council Summit Pledges to Continue Strengthening Activities for Maintenance of International Peace, Security," press release (New York, NY, September 23, 2010), http://www.un.org/News/Press/docs/2010/sc10036.doc.htm.

7. Nassir Abdulaziz Al-Nasser, "Remarks at the Informal Discussion on United Nations Mediation" (New York, NY, November 9, 2011), http://www.un.org/en/ga/president/66/statements/mediation091111.shtml.

8. Nassir Abdulaziz Al-Nasser, "On the Occasion of the Establishment and First Meeting of the Advisory Board of the Special Human Settlements Programme for the Palestinian People" (New York, NY, February 8, 2012), http://www.un.org/en/ga/president/66/statements/palestine080212.shtml.

9. Al-Nasser, "On the Occasion of the Breakfast Meeting."

10. Al-Nasser, "On the Occasion of the International Istanbul Conference." For the president's summary of the event, see http://www.un.org/en/ga/president/66/Letters/PDF/Mediation%20Summary%20-%2023%20November%202011.pdf.

11. Al-Nasser, "On the Occasion of the Breakfast Meeting."

12. Al-Nasser, "On the Occasion of the International Istanbul Conference."

13. Nassir Abdulaziz Al-Nasser, "At the Opening of the Interactive Thematic Debate on Fostering Cross-Cultural Understanding for Building Peaceful and Inclusive Societies" (United Nations, New York, NY, March 22, 2012), http://www.un.org/en/ga/president/66/statements/cultural220312.shtml.

14. Nassir Abdulaziz Al-Nasser, "Remarks at the Partners Forum of the United Nations Alliance of Civilizations" (Istanbul, Turkey, May 31, 2012), http://www.un.org/en/ga/president/66/statements/allianceofciv310512.shtml.

15. United Nations General Assembly Resolution 64/14, "The Alliance of Civiliza-

tions," November 10, 2009, http://www.un.org/en/ga/search/view_doc.asp?symbol =A/RES/64/14.

16. Al-Nasser, "At the Opening of the Interactive Thematic Debate."

17. Nassir Abdulaziz Al-Nasser, "On the Occasion of the Ministerial Meeting of the Group of Friends of the UN Alliance of Civilizations" (New York, NY, September 23, 2011), http://www.un.org/en/ga/president/66/statements/allianceofciv230911 .shtml. For the sixth and most recent report of the UNAOC high representative, see http://www.unaoc.org/wp-content/uploads/Draft22August2013-UNAOC -Sixth-Annual-Report.pdf.

18. Al-Nasser, "At the Opening of the Interactive Thematic Debate."

19. Al-Nasser, "On the Occasion of the Ministerial Meeting of the Group of Friends."

20. Al-Nasser, "At the Opening of the Interactive Thematic Debate."

21. Nassir Abdulaziz Al-Nasser, "Remarks on the Occasion of the Fourth Forum of the United Nations Alliance of Civilizations" (Doha, Qatar, December 11, 2011), http:// www.un.org/en/ga/president/66/statements/allianceofciv111211.shtml.

22. Al-Nasser, "On the Occasion of the Ministerial Meeting of the Group of Friends."

23. Nassir Abdulaziz Al-Nasser, "Remarks on the Occasion of World Interfaith Harmony Week 'Common Ground for the Common Good'" (New York, NY, February 7, 2012), http://www.un.org/en/ga/president/66/statements/harmonyweek070212 .shtml.

24. Nassir Abdulaziz Al-Nasser, "At the Closing of the Interactive Thematic Debate on Fostering Cross-Cultural Understanding for Building Peaceful and Inclusive Societies" (United Nations, New York, NY, March 22, 2012), http://www.un.org/en/ ga/president/66/statements/cultural22032012.shtml.

25. Al-Nasser, "Remarks on the Occasion of World Interfaith Harmony Week."

26. Al-Nasser, "On the Occasion of the International Istanbul Conference."

27. Al-Nasser, "Opening Remarks . . . on the Role of the Member States in Mediation."

28. Nassir Abdulaziz Al-Nasser, "Closing Remarks at the High Level Meeting of the General Assembly on the Role of the Member States in Mediation" (New York, NY, May 23, 2012), http://www.un.org/en/ga/president/66/statements/mediation 23052012.shtml.

29. Al-Nasser, "Opening Remarks . . . on the Role of the Member States in Mediation."

NOTES TO CHAPTER 3

1. Nassir Abdulaziz Al-Nasser, "Opening Remarks at the General Assembly Retreat on Security Council Reform" (Glen Cove, NY, March 30, 2012), http://www.un.org/ en/ga/president/66/statements/scrretreat300312.shtml.

2. Platform for Change, "Security Council Reform Platforms," http://pfcun.org/ Platforms.html.

3. Han Seung-soo, *Beyond the Shadow of 9/11: A Year at the United Nations General Assembly* (Washington, DC: Edwin O. Reischauer Center for East Asian Studies, Johns Hopkins University–SAIS, 2007), 103.

4. Nassir Abdulaziz Al-Nasser, "On the Occasion of the Tokyo Dialogue on Security Council Reform" (Tokyo, Japan, November 14, 2011), http://www.un.org/en/ga/president/66/statements/tokyodialogue141111.shtml.

5. United Nations General Assembly Resolution 60/1, "2005 World Summit Outcome" (New York, NY, October 24, 2005), http://daccess-dds-ny.un.org/doc/UNDOC/GEN/N05/487/60/PDF/N0548760.pdf?OpenElement.

6. United Nations General Assembly, "Resolutions and Decisions Adopted by the General Assembly During Its Sixty-Second Session: Volume III" (New York, NY, 2008), 106, http://www.un.org/ga/search/view_doc.asp?symbol=a/62/49(vol.III)&Lang=E.

7. Nassir Abdulaziz Al-Nasser, "Remarks at the Plenary Meeting of the United Nations General Assembly on Agenda Item 122" (New York, NY, November 8, 2011), http://www.un.org/en/ga/president/66/statements/item122sc081111.shtml.

8. Al-Nasser, "On the Occasion of the Tokyo Dialogue."

9. Al-Nasser, "Opening Remarks at the General Assembly Retreat."

10. Han Seung-soo, *Beyond the Shadow of 9/11*, 65.

11. Nassir Abdulaziz Al-Nasser, "Closing Remarks at the General Assembly Retreat on Security Council Reform" (Glen Cove, NY, March 31, 2012), http://www.un.org/en/ga/president/66/statements/scrretreat310312.shtml.

12. Nassir Abdulaziz Al-Nasser, "Remarks on Agenda Item 121: Revitalization of the Work of the General Assembly" (New York, NY, December 1, 2011), http://www.un.org/en/ga/president/66/statements/revitalization011211.shtml.

13. Nassir Abdulaziz Al-Nasser, "First Meeting of the Ad Hoc Working Group on the Revitalization of the Work of the General Assembly" (New York, NY, March 27, 2012), http://www.un.org/en/ga/president/66/statements/revitalization270312.shtml.

14. Han Seung-soo, *Beyond the Shadow of 9/11*, 106–107.

15. Al-Nasser, "Remarks on Agenda Item 121."

16. Han Seung-soo, *Beyond the Shadow of 9/11*, 99.

17. Nassir Abdulaziz Al-Nasser, "Remarks on the Presentation of the Security Council Report" (New York, NY, November 8, 2011), http://www.un.org/en/ga/president/66/statements/screport081111.shtml.

18. Al-Nasser, "Remarks on Agenda Item 121."

19. United Nations General Assembly Resolution 66/253, "The Situation in the Syrian Arab Republic," February 21, 2012, http://www.un.org/ga/search/view_doc.asp?symbol=%20A/RES/66/253.

20. Al-Nasser, "First Meeting of the Ad Hoc Working Group."

21. Nassir Abdulaziz Al-Nasser, "Remarks to the Ad Hoc Working Group on the Revitalization of the General Assembly" (New York, NY, June 1, 2012), http://www.un.org/en/ga/president/66/statements/revitalization010612.shtml.

22. Al-Nasser, "First Meeting of the Ad Hoc Working Group."

23. United Nations General Assembly Resolution 66/246, "Questions Relating to the

Proposed Programme Budget for the Biennium 2012–2013," February 29, 2012, http://www.un.org/ga/search/view_doc.asp?symbol=%20A/RES/66/246.

24. Al-Nasser, "Remarks to the Ad Hoc Working Group."

25. Nassir Abdulaziz Al-Nasser, "Message from the President at the ECOSOC 2011 Retreat on 'Enhancing the Role of ECOSOC'" (Manhasset, NY, November 11, 2011), http://www.un.org/en/ga/president/66/statements/ecosocretreat111111.shtml.

NOTES TO CHAPTER 4

1. Nassir Abdulaziz Al-Nasser, "Message to the Arab Aid Consortium" (Kuwait, March 12, 2012), http://www.un.org/en/ga/president/66/statements/arabaid120312 .shtml.

2. Nassir Abdulaziz Al-Nasser, "On the Occasion of the Mini-Summit on the Humanitarian Response to the Horn of Africa" (New York, NY, September 24, 2011), http://www.un.org/en/ga/president/66/statements/africa240911.shtml. See also United Nations General Assembly Resolution 66/120, "Strengthening Humanitarian Assistance, Emergency Relief and Rehabilitation in Response to Severe Drought in the Horn of Africa Region," March 7, 2012, http://www.un.org/ ga/search/view_doc.asp?symbol=%20A/RES/66/120.

3. Nassir Abdulaziz Al-Nasser, "Remarks on the Joint Visit of the President of the General Assembly and the Secretary-General to Somalia" (New York, NY, December 21, 2011), http://www.un.org/en/ga/president/66/statements/somaliabriefing 211211.shtml.

4. United Nations Security Council Resolution 2036 (2012), adopted by the Security Council at its 6,718th meeting, on February 22, 2012, http://www.un.org/ga/search/ view_doc.asp?symbol=S/RES/2036(2012).

5. Nassir Abdulaziz Al-Nasser, "Remarks at the Istanbul Conference on Somalia" (Istanbul, Turkey, June 1, 2012), http://www.un.org/en/ga/president/66/statements/ istanbulconf010612.shtml.

6. United Nations General Assembly Resolution 65/307, "Improving the Effectiveness and Coordination of Military and Civil Defence Assets for Natural Disaster Response," August 25, 2011, http://www.un.org/ga/search/view_doc.asp?symbol= A/RES/65/307.

7. Nassir Abdulaziz Al-Nasser, "Before the International Conference on the HOPEFOR Initiative" (Doha, Qatar, November 29, 2011), http://www.un.org/en/ ga/president/66/statements/hopefor291111.shtml.

NOTES TO CHAPTER 5

1. Nassir Abdulaziz Al-Nasser, "Opening Remarks: Briefing to Member States on the Report of the High-Level Panel on Global Sustainability" (New York, NY, October 20, 2011), http://www.un.org/en/ga/president/66/statements/openingremarks -20102011.shtml.

2. Nassir Abdulaziz Al-Nasser, "At the Press Conference Marking the Day of 7

Billion" (New York, NY, October 31, 2011), http://www.un.org/en/ga/president/66/statements/7billionremarks-311011.shtml.

3. Nations Conference on Environment and Development, Johannesburg Summit 2002, http://www.un.org/jsummit/html/basic_info/unced.html.

4. Nassir Abdulaziz Al-Nasser, "On the Occasion of the Second Committee Side Event, 'Means of Implementation of Sustainable Development'" (New York, NY, October 25, 2011), http://www.un.org/en/ga/president/66/statements/secondcom side251011.shtml.

5. Nassir Abdulaziz Al-Nasser, "On the Occasion of the Second Committee Meeting on Sustainable Development (Agenda 19)" (New York, NY, October 31, 2011), http://www.un.org/en/ga/president/66/statements/secondcommtg311011.shtml.

6. Nassir Abdulaziz Al-Nasser, "On the Occasion of the Opening of the High-Level Meeting on 'Addressing Desertification, Land Degradation and Drought in the Context of Sustainable Development and Poverty Eradication'" (New York, NY, September 20, 2011), http://www.un.org/en/ga/president/66/statements/desertificationopening20092011.shtml.

7. IISD Reporting Services, "UNCCD COP 10 Adopts Decisions on GM Governance, Scientific Advice and Indicators," http://climate-l.iisd.org/news/unccd-cop-10-adopts-decisions-on-gm-governance-scientific-advice-and-indicators/.

8. United Nations Conference on Trade and Development, "Who We Are" (Geneva, Switzerland, 2013), http://unctad.org/en/Pages/AboutUs.aspx.

9. Nassir Abdulaziz Al-Nasser, "Remarks on the Occasion of the Handover Ceremony of the Chairmanship of the Group of 77" (New York, NY, January 11, 2012), http://www.un.org/en/ga/president/66/statements/group77-110112.shtml.

10. Nassir Abdulaziz Al-Nasser, "Remarks at the Joint Press Conference with the Secretary-General of UNCTAD" (Doha, Qatar, April 20, 2012), http://www.un.org/en/ga/president/66/statements/unctad200412.shtml.

11. Nassir Abdulaziz Al-Nasser, "Remarks at the High-Level Segment of the Economic and Social Council" (New York, NY, July 2, 2012), http://www.un.org/en/ga/president/66/statements/ecosoco20712.shtml.

12. Al-Nasser, "Opening Remarks: Briefing to Member States."

13. Al-Nasser, "On the Occasion of the Second Committee Side Event."

14. Nassir Abdulaziz Al-Nasser, "On the Occasion of the International Day for the Eradication of Poverty" (New York, NY, October 15, 2011), http://www.un.org/en/ga/president/66/statements/poverty151011.shtml.

15. United Nations Food and Agriculture Organization, "About FAO," http://www.fao.org/about/en/.

16. Nassir Abdulaziz Al-Nasser, "On the Occasion of World Food Day 2011" (New York, NY, October 27, 2011), http://www.un.org/en/ga/president/66/statements/worldfoodday27102011.shtml.

17. Nassir Abdulaziz Al-Nasser, "Remarks on the Occasion of the Adoption of the

Resolution Entitled, 'Addressing Excessive Price Volatility in Food and Related Financial and Commodity Markets' " (Santo Domingo, Dominican Republic, December 27, 2011), http://www.un.org/en/ga/president/66/statements/foodprice 271211.shtml.

18. United Nations General Assembly Resolution 66/188, "Addressing Excessive Price Volatility in Food and Related Financial and Commodity Markets," February 14, 2012, http://www.un.org/ga/search/view_doc.asp?symbol=%20A/RES/66/188.

19. Nassir Abdulaziz Al-Nasser, "Opening Remarks at the High-Level Thematic Debate on Addressing Excessive Price Volatility in Food and Related Commodity Markets" (New York, NY, April 11, 2012), http://www.un.org/en/ga/president/66/ statements/pricevolatility110412.shtml.

20. United Nations General Assembly, President of the 65th Session, "Sustainable Development," http://www.un.org/en/ga/president/65/issues/sustdev.shtml.

21. International Decade for Action "Water for Life" 2005–2015, "About the Decade," https://www.un.org/waterforlifedecade/background.shtml.

22. Nassir Abdulaziz Al-Nasser, "Remarks on the Occasion of the Side Event: 'From the World Water Day, 2012 "Water and Food Security" to International Year Water Cooperation 2013': Celebration of the International Water Day" (New York, NY, March 22, 2012), http://www.un.org/en/ga/president/66/statements/water220312 .shtml.

23. Al-Nasser, "On the Occasion of the Opening of the High-Level Meeting on 'Addressing Desertification.' "

24. Han Seung-soo, *Beyond the Shadow of 9/11: A Year at the United Nations General Assembly* (Washington, DC: Edwin O. Reischauer Center for East Asian Studies, Johns Hopkins University–SAIS, 2007), 51.

25. United Nations General Assembly Resolution 65/160, "Implementation of the United Nations Convention to Combat Desertification in Those Countries Experiencing Serious Drought and/or Desertification, Particularly in Africa," March 4, 2011, http://www.un.org/ga/search/view_doc.asp?symbol=A/RES/65/160.

26. Nassir Abdulaziz Al-Nasser, "On the Occasion of the Tenth Meeting of the Conference of the Parties to the United Nations Convention to Combat Desertification" (Republic of Korea, October 13, 2011), http://www.un.org/en/ga/president/66/ statements/korea131011.shtml.

27. Al-Nasser, "On the Occasion of the Second Committee Meeting on Sustainable Development (Agenda 19)."

28. Nassir Abdulaziz Al-Nasser, "On the Occasion of the United Nations Private Sector Forum on Sustainable Energy for All" (New York, NY, September 20, 2011), http://www.un.org/en/ga/president/66/statements/energy20092011.shtml.

29. Nassir Abdulaziz Al-Nasser, "Remarks at the Fifth World Future Energy Summit" (Abu Dhabi, UAE, January 16, 2012), http://www.un.org/en/ga/president/66/ statements/energysummit160112.shtml. See also United Nations General Assembly

Resolution 65/151, "International Year of Sustainable Energy for All," February 16, 2011, http://www.un.org/ga/search/view_doc.asp?symbol=A/RES/65/151.

30. International Renewable Energy Agency, "About IRENA," http://www.irena.org/Menu/index.aspx?PriMenuID=13&mnu=Pri.

31. World Future Energy Summit (Abu Dhabi, United Arab Emirates), http://www.worldfutureenergysummit.com/.

32. Nassir Abdulaziz Al-Nasser, "Remarks at the Foreign Policy Association 'The Future of Energy Conference'" (New York, NY, May 24, 2012), http://www.un.org/en/ga/president/66/statements/energy240512.shtml.

33. Al-Nasser, "Remarks at the Fifth World Future Energy Summit."

34. Nassir Abdulaziz Al-Nasser, "The Interactive Dialogue on Harmony with Nature to Commemorate International Mother Earth Day" (New York, NY, April 18, 2012), http://www.un.org/en/ga/president/66/statements/harmony180412.shtml.

35. Nassir Abdulaziz Al-Nasser, "On the Occasion of the High-Level Meeting on the Yasuni Initiative" (New York, NY, September 23, 2011), http://www.un.org/en/ga/president/66/statements/yasuni230911.shtml.

36. Nassir Abdulaziz Al-Nasser, "On the Occasion of the World Habitat Day 2011 Observance" (New York, NY, October 3, 2011), http://www.un.org/en/ga/president/66/statements/worldhabitato31011.shtml.

37. United Nations General Assembly Resolution 66/204, "Harmony with Nature," March 29, 2012, http://www.un.org/ga/search/view_doc.asp?symbol=%20A/RES/66/204.

38. Al-Nasser, "The Interactive Dialogue on Harmony with Nature."

39. Al-Nasser, "On the Occasion of the Second Committee Meeting on Sustainable Development (Agenda 19)."

40. Convention on Biological Diversity, "The Nagoya Protocol on Access and Benefit-Sharing," http://www.cbd.int/abs/.

41. Convention on Biological Diversity, "The Nagoya-Kuala Lumpur Supplementary Protocol on Liability and Redress to the Cartagena Protocol on Biosafety," http://bch.cbd.int/protocol/NKL_pressrelease.shtml.

42. United Nations Office on Drugs and Crime, "World Drug Report 2012" (New York, NY, June 2012), http://www.unodc.org/documents/data-and-analysis/WDR2012/WDR_2012_web_small.pdf.

43. United Nations, Conferences, Meetings and Events, "The 2005 World Summit High-Level Plenary Meeting of the 60th Session of the UN General Assembly" (UN Headquarters, New York, NY, September 14–16, 2005), http://www.un.org/en/events/pastevents/worldsummit_2005.shtml.

44. Nassir Abdulaziz Al-Nasser, "Opening Remarks at the Thematic Debate of the General Assembly on Drugs and Crime as a Threat to Development" (New York, NY, June 26, 2012), http://www.un.org/en/ga/president/66/statements/drugscrime250612.shtml.

45. United Nations General Assembly Resolution 65/94, "The United Nations in

Global Governance," January 28, 2011, http://www.un.org/ga/search/view_doc.asp?symbol=A/RES/65/294.

46. United Nations General Assembly, "Global Economic Governance and Development: Report of the Secretary-General" (A/66/506), October 10, 2011, http://www.un.org/ga/search/view_doc.asp?symbol=A/66/506.

47. Russia G20, "What Is the G20?," http://www.g20.org/docs/about/about_G20.html.

48. G8 Information Centre, "What Is the G8?" (University of Toronto, 2013), http://www.g8.utoronto.ca/what_is_g8.html.

49. Iftekhar Ahmed Chowdhury, "The Global Governance Group ('3G') and Singaporean Leadership" (Institute of South Asian Studies, May 19, 2010), http://www.isn.ethz.ch/Digital-Library/Publications/Detail/?ots591=0c54e3b3-1e9c-be1e-2c24-a6a8c7060233&lng=en&id=116447.

50. Nassir Abdulaziz Al-Nasser, "Remarks on the Occasion of Item 123(B) 'Central Role of the United Nations System in Global Governance' " (New York, NY, December 16, 2011), http://www.un.org/en/ga/president/66/statements/global governance161211.shtml.

51. United Nations General Assembly Resolution 66/256, "The United Nations in Global Governance," May 15, 2012, http://www.un.org/ga/search/view_doc.asp?symbol=%20A/RES/66/256.

52. Nassir Abdulaziz Al-Nasser, "Opening Remarks at the High-Level Thematic Debate on the State of the World Economy and Finance and Its Impact on Development in 2012" (New York, NY, May 17, 2012), http://www.un.org/en/ga/president/66/statements/economy170512.shtml.

53. Nassir Abdulaziz Al-Nasser, "Closing Remarks at the High-Level Thematic Debate on the State of the World Economy and Finance and Its Impact on Development in 2012" (New York, NY, May 18, 2012), http://www.un.org/en/ga/president/66/statements/economy180512.shtml.

54. Nassir Abdulaziz Al-Nasser, "Letter Dated 22 June to All Permanent Missions and Permanent Observer Missions to the United Nations" (New York, NY, June 22, 2012), http://www.un.org/en/ga/president/66/Letters/PDF/Economic%20Crisis%20letter%20from%20SG%20and%20PGA%20and%20Summary%20-%2022%20June%202012.pdf.

55. Nassir Abdulaziz Al-Nasser, "Remarks at the 10th Annual International Forum of the Convention of Independent Financial Advisors" (Monaco, April 25, 2012), http://www.un.org/en/ga/president/66/statements/cifa250412.shtml.

56. Al-Nasser, "Remarks at the High-Level Segment of the Economic and Social Council."

57. Al-Nasser, "Remarks at the Joint Press Conference with the Secretary-General of UNCTAD."

58. UN Office of the High Representative for the Least Developed Countries, Landlocked Developing Countries, and Small Island Developing States, "About LDCs," http://unohrlls.org/about-ldcs/about-ldcs/.

59. UN Office of the High Representative for the Least Developed Countries, Land-locked Developing Countries, and Small Island Developing States, "The Criteria for Identification of the LDCs," http://www.un.org/special-rep/ohrlls/ldc/ldc%20 criteria.htm.

60. United Nations, "List of Least Developed Countries," http://www.un.org/esa/ policy/devplan/profile/ldc_list.pdf.

61. Nassir Abdulaziz Al-Nasser, "Opening Remarks on the Occasion of the Fifth High-Level Dialogue on Financing for Development" (New York, NY, December 7, 2011), http://www.un.org/en/ga/president/66/statements/financing071211.shtml.

62. "United Nations Development Assistance Framework," *Wikipedia*, http:// en.wikipedia.org/wiki/United_Nations_Development_Assistance_Framework.

63. United Nations Development Group, "Resident Coordinator System," http://www .undg.org/content/resident_coordinator_system_1_1.

64. United Nations General Assembly Resolution 32/197, "Restructuring of the Economic and Social Sectors of the United Nations System," December 19, 1977, http:// www.un.org/ga/search/view_doc.asp?symbol=A/RES/32/197&Lang=E&Area= RESOLUTION.

65. Nassir Abdulaziz Al-Nasser, "Welcome Remarks at the Tarrytown Retreat for the Dialogue on UN Operational Activities for Development" (Tarrytown, NY, June 8, 2012), http://www.un.org/en/ga/president/66/statements/tarrytownretreat080612 .shtml.

66. Nassir Abdulaziz Al-Nasser, "Closing Remarks at the Tarrytown Retreat for the Dialogue on UN Operational Activities for Development" (Tarrytown, NY, June 9, 2012), http://www.un.org/en/ga/president/66/statements/tarrytownretreat090612 .shtml.

67. United Nations General Assembly Resolution 64/222, "Nairobi Outcome Document of the High-Level United Nations Conference on South-South Cooperation," February 23, 2010, http://ssc.undp.org/content/dam/ssc/documents/GA%20 Resolutions/GA%20Resolution%202009.pdf.

68. Nassir Abdulaziz Al-Nasser, "Remarks at the Opening of the 17th Session of the High-Level Committee on South-South Cooperation" (New York, NY, May 22, 2012), http://www.un.org/en/ga/president/66/statements/southsouth220512.shtml.

69. Nassir Abdulaziz Al-Nasser, "On the Occasion of the Opening Ceremony of the Global South-South Development Expo 2011" (Rome, Italy, December 5, 2011), http://www.un.org/en/ga/president/66/statements/gssdexpo051211.shtml.

70. The LDC Civil Society Forum, "Istanbul Declaration," May 13, 2011, http://www.un .org/wcm/content/site/ldc/home/pid/17029.

71. Nassir Abdulaziz Al-Nasser, "On the Occasion of the Annual Ministerial Meeting of the Least Developed Countries" (New York, NY, September 26, 2011), http:// www.un.org/en/ga/president/66/statements/ldcministerial260911.shtml.

72. United Nations General Assembly Resolution 66/213, "Fourth United Nations

Conference on the Least Developed Countries," March 26, 2012, http://www.un
.org/ga/search/view_doc.asp?symbol=%20A/RES/66/213.

73. Nassir Abdulaziz Al-Nasser, "Remarks on the Ad Hoc Working Group of the General Assembly on the Smooth Transition of the LDCs" (New York, NY, December
22, 2011), http://www.un.org/en/ga/president/66/statements/ldcs221211.shtml.

74. Han Seung-soo, *Beyond the Shadow of 9/11*, 86.

75. Nassir Abdulaziz Al-Nasser, "Remarks at the Side Event on 'LDCs and RIO+20'
during the UN Conference on Sustainable Development" (Rio de Janeiro,
Brazil, June 21, 2012), http://www.un.org/en/ga/president/66/statements/rio20
sideevent210612.shtml.

76. Al-Nasser, "Remarks on the Ad Hoc Working Group."

77. UN Office of the High Representative for the Least Developed Countries, Landlocked Developing Countries, and Small Island Developing States, "About SIDS,"
http://unohrlls.org/about-sids/.

78. UN Office of the High Representative for the Least Developed Countries, Landlocked Developing Countries, and Small Island Developing States, "Landlocked
Developing Countries," http://www.un.org/special-rep/ohrlls/lldc/default.htm.

79. United Nations General Assembly Resolution 56.227, "Third United Nations Conference on the Least Developed Countries," February 28, 2002, http://www.un.org/
ga/search/view_doc.asp?symbol=A/RES/56/227&Lang=E.

80. Al-Nasser, "Remarks at the Side Event on 'LDCs and RIO+20.'"

81. Al-Nasser, "On the Occasion of the Annual Ministerial Meeting of the Least
Developed Countries."

82. United Nations General Assembly Resolution 66/293, "A Monitoring Mechanism
to Review Commitments Made towards Africa's Development," October 15, 2012,
http://www.un.org/ga/search/view_doc.asp?symbol=%20A/RES/66/293.

83. Nassir Abdulaziz Al-Nasser, "On the Occasion of the High-Level Event to Mark
10 Years of NEPAD" (New York, NY, October 7, 2011), http://www.un.org/en/ga/
president/66/statements/nepad071011.shtml.

84. Nassir Abdulaziz Al-Nasser, "Remarks on the Occasion of African Industrialization Day 2011" (New York, NY, November 22, 2011), http://www.un.org/en/ga/
president/66/statements/africanindustrialization221111.shtml.

85. United Nations Conference on Sustainable Development (Rio+20), "Outcome of
the Conference," June 19, 2012, http://daccess-dds-ny.un.org/doc/UNDOC/GEN/
N12/381/64/PDF/N1238164.pdf?OpenElement.

86. Andre Skowronski, "Aquas de Marco Antonio Carlos Jobim Lyrics," *Belavistario*
.com, March 1, 2009, http://www.belavistario.com/blog/item/2009/03/aquas-de
-marco-antonio-carlos-jobim-lyrics/catid/13.

87. Nassir Abdulaziz Al-Nasser, "Remarks at the United Nations Conference on
Sustainable Development (Rio+20)" (Rio De Janeiro, Brazil, June 20, 2012), http://
www.un.org/en/ga/president/66/statements/rio20conf200612.shtml.

88. Al-Nasser, "Remarks at the High-Level Segment of the Economic and Social Council."

89. Nassir Abdulaziz Al-Nasser, "Remarks at the Informal Briefing on Secretary-General's Global Pulse Initiative" (New York, NY, November 8, 2011), http://www.un.org/en/ga/president/66/statements/globalpulse081111.shtml.

90. Nassir Abdulaziz Al-Nasser, "Remarks at the United Nations General Assembly Event to Commemorate the 25th Anniversary of the United Nations Declaration on the Right to Development" (New York, NY, November 8, 2011), http://www.un.org/en/ga/president/66/statements/development25th81111.shtml.

91. Nassir Abdulaziz Al-Nasser, "On the Occasion of the 2011 Forum on Diaspora Economy" (New York, NY, December 2, 2011), http://www.un.org/en/ga/president/66/statements/diaspora021211.shtml.

92. United Nations General Assembly Resolution 65/309, "Happiness: Towards a Holistic Approach to Development," August 25, 2011, http://www.un.org/ga/search/view_doc.asp?symbol=A/RES/65/309.

93. Nassir Abdulaziz Al-Nasser, "Remarks at the High-Level Meeting on Well-Being and Happiness" (New York, NY, April 2, 2012), http://www.un.org/en/ga/president/66/statements/happiness020412.shtml.

94. Nassir Abdulaziz Al-Nasser, "On the Occasion of International Women's Day" (New York, NY, March 7, 2012), http://www.un.org/en/ga/president/66/statements/women070312.shtml.

NOTES TO CHAPTER 6

1. Nassir Abdulaziz Al-Nasser, "Plenary Meeting of the General Assembly Debate on the Report of the Secretary-General: 'Follow-Up to Resolution 64/291 on Human Security'" (New York, NY, June 4, 2012), http://www.un.org/en/ga/president/66/statements/humansecurity040612.shtml.

2. Nassir Abdulaziz Al-Nasser, "Remarks of the President of the General Assembly on the Occasion of Human Rights Day" (New York, NY, December 9, 2011), http://www.un.org/en/ga/president/66/statements/humanrightsday091211.shtml. See also Charter of the United Nations, chapter 9, "International Economic and Social Co-Operation," http://www.un.org/en/documents/charter/chapter9.shtml.

3. United Nations Human Rights, Office of the High Commissioner for Human Rights, "Basic Facts about the UPR," http://www.ohchr.org/en/hrbodies/upr/pages/BasicFacts.aspx.

4. Nassir Abdulaziz Al-Nasser, "Remarks at the Plenary Meeting of the General Assembly on Agenda Item 64: 'Report of the Human Rights Council'" (New York, NY, November 2, 2011), http://www.un.org/en/ga/president/66/statements/hrc021111.shtml.

5. United Nations General Assembly Resolution 66/254, "Intergovernmental Process of the General Assembly on Strengthening and Enhancing the Effective

Functioning of the Human Rights Treaty Body System," May 15, 2012, http://www
.un.org/ga/search/view_doc.asp?symbol=%20A/RES/66/254.

6. Nassir Abdulaziz Al-Nasser, "Remarks at the Treaty Body Strengthening Consultation for States Parties to International Human Rights Treaties" (New York, NY,
April 2, 2012), http://www.un.org/en/ga/president/66/statements/humanrights
020412.shtml.

7. Nassir Abdulaziz Al-Nasser, "Opening Remarks at the High-Level Meeting on the
Prevention and Control of Non-communicable Diseases" (New York, NY, September 19, 2011), http://www.un.org/en/ga/president/66/statements/ncds19092011
.shtml.

8. Nassir Abdulaziz Al-Nasser, "On the Occasion of the First Meeting of UN Funds,
Programmes and Agencies on the Implementation of the Political Declaration of
the High-Level Meeting of the General Assembly on the Prevention and Control of
Non-communicable Diseases" (New York, NY, December 8, 2011), http://www.un
.org/en/ga/president/66/statements/ncds081211.shtml.

9. Nassir Abdulaziz Al-Nasser, "Opening Remarks at the Second Meeting of UN
Funds, Programmes and Agencies on the Implementation of the Political Declaration of the High-Level Meeting of the General Assembly on the Prevention and
Control of Non-communicable Diseases" (New York, NY, June 29, 2012), http://
www.un.org/en/ga/president/66/statements/ncds290612.shtml.

10. Nassir Abdulaziz Al-Nasser, "South-South Awards 2011: Digital Health for Digital
Development" (New York, NY, September 19, 2011), http://www.un.org/en/ga/
president/66/statements/southsouthawards19092011.shtml.

11. Nassir Abdulaziz Al-Nasser, "Remarks at the Plenary Meeting on the Implementation of the Declaration of Commitments on HIV/AIDS and the Political Declaration on HIV/AIDS" (New York, NY, June 11, 2012), http://www.un.org/en/ga/
president/66/statements/hivaids110612.shtml.

12. United Nations, "Convention on the Rights of Persons with Disabilities," December 13, 2006, http://www.un.org/disabilities/default.asp?id=259.

13. Nassir Abdulaziz Al-Nasser, "On the Occasion of the Commemoration of the
International Day of Persons with Disabilities" (New York, NY, December 2, 2011),
http://www.un.org/en/ga/president/66/statements/disabilities021211.shtml.

14. United Nations General Assembly Resolution 62/139, "World Autism Awareness
Day," January 21, 2008, http://www.un.org/ga/search/view_doc.asp?symbol=A/
RES/62/139&Lang=E.

15. Nassir Abdulaziz Al-Nasser, "Remarks on the Occasion of World Autism Day"
(New York, NY, April 3, 2012), http://www.un.org/en/ga/president/66/statements/
autism030412.shtml.

16. Al-Nasser, "On the Occasion of the Commemoration of the International Day of
Persons with Disabilities."

17. United Nations World Conference against Racism, Racial Discrimination,

Xenophobia and Related Intolerance, "Durban Declaration and Programme of Action," September 8, 2001, http://www.un.org/durbanreview2009/pdf/DDPA_full_text.pdf.

18. Nassir Abdulaziz Al-Nasser, "On the Occasion of the Opening of the HLM to Commemorate the Tenth Anniversary of the Durban Declaration and Programme of Action" (New York, NY, September 22, 2011), http://www.un.org/en/ga/president/66/statements/durban220901.shtml.

19. Nassir Abdulaziz Al-Nasser, "On the Occasion of the Closing of the HLM to Commemorate the Tenth Anniversary of the Durban Declaration and Programme of Action" (New York, NY, September 22, 2011), http://www.un.org/en/ga/president/66/statements/durbancl220901.shtml.

20. International Organization for Migration, "About IOM," http://www.iom.int/cms/about-iom.

21. United Nations, "Declaration on the Rights of Indigenous Peoples," March 2008, http://www.un.org/esa/socdev/unpfii/documents/DRIPS_en.pdf.

22. United Nations General Assembly Resolution 65/198, "Indigenous Issues," March 3, 2011, http://www.un.org/ga/search/view_doc.asp?symbol=A/RES/65/198.

23. Nassir Abdulaziz Al-Nasser, "Remarks at the High-Level Event to Commemorate the 5th Anniversary of the Adoption of the UN Declaration on the Rights of Indigenous Peoples" (New York, NY, May 17, 2012), http://www.un.org/en/ga/president/66/statements/indigenous170512.shtml.

24. United Nations General Assembly Resolution 64/293, "United Nations Global Plan of Action to Combat Trafficking in Persons," August 12, 2010, http://www.un.org/ga/search/view_doc.asp?symbol=A/RES/64/293.

25. Nassir Abdulaziz Al-Nasser, "On the Occasion of the Second Ministerial Meeting of the Group of Friends United Against Human Trafficking" (New York, NY, September 26, 2011), http://www.un.org/en/ga/president/66/statements/trafficking260911.shtml.

26. United Nations Secretariat, "Special Measures for Protection from Sexual Exploitation and Sexual Abuse," October 9, 2003, http://daccess-dds-ny.un.org/doc/UNDOC/GEN/N03/550/40/PDF/N0355040.pdf?OpenElement.

27. Nassir Abdulaziz Al-Nasser, "On the Occasion of the Interactive Dialogue on Human Trafficking: Partnership and Innovation to End Violence against Women & Girls" (New York, NY, April 3, 2012), http://www.un.org/en/ga/president/66/statements/trafficking030412.shtml.

28. Nassir Abdulaziz Al-Nasser, "Concert in Support of a Permanent Memorial to Honour the Victims of Slavery and the Transatlantic Slave Trade at United Nations Headquarters" (New York, NY, May 15, 2012), http://www.un.org/en/ga/president/66/statements/slaveryconcert150512.shtml.

29. Nassir Abdulaziz Al-Nasser, "On the Occasion of the Commemoration of International Day of Remembrance of the Victims of Slavery and the Transatlantic Slave

Trade" (New York, NY, March 23, 2012), http://www.un.org/en/ga/president/66/statements/slavetrade260312.shtml.

30. United Nations Office on Drugs and Crime, "UN Task Force on Transnational Organized Crime and Drug Trafficking Enters New Phase with Tajikistan Regional Meeting" (Dushanbe, Tajikistan, June 1, 2012), http://www.unodc.org/unodc/en/press/releases/2012/June/un-task-force-on-transnational-organized-crime-and-drug-trafficking-enters-new-phase-with-tajikistan-regional-meeting.html.

31. Nassir Abdulaziz Al-Nasser, "On the Occasion of the 21st Session of the Commission on Crime Prevention and Criminal Justice" (Vienna, Austria, April 23, 2012), http://www.un.org/en/ga/president/66/statements/crimeprevention230412.shtml.

32. Central American Security Commission, "Central American Security Strategy" (San Salvador, El Salvador, June 2011), http://www.europarl.europa.eu/meetdocs/2009_2014/documents/dcam/dv/ca_security_s_/ca_security_s_en.pdf.

33. Nassir Abdulaziz Al-Nasser, "Opening Remarks at the Thematic Debate of the General Assembly on Security in Central America as a Regional and Global Challenge" (New York, NY, May 16, 2012), http://www.un.org/en/ga/president/66/statements/sica160512.shtml.

34. Nassir Abdulaziz Al-Nasser, "Closing Remarks at the Thematic Debate of the General Assembly on Security in Central America as a Regional and Global Challenge" (New York, NY, May 16, 2012), http://www.un.org/en/ga/president/66/statements/sicaclosing160512.shtml.

35. Nassir Abdulaziz Al-Nasser, "On the Occasion of the Memorial Event Paying Tribute to Fallen UN Colleagues" (New York, NY, November 21, 2011), http://www.un.org/en/ga/president/66/statements/memorial21111121.shtml.

36. Nassir Abdulaziz Al-Nasser, "Address to the Special Committee on Peacekeeping Operations (C-34)" (New York, NY, February 21, 2012), http://www.un.org/en/ga/president/66/statements/pko210212.shtml.

37. Nassir Abdulaziz Al-Nasser, "On the Occasion of the High-Level Briefing on 'Broadening the Concept of Peacekeeping: The Contribution of Civil Society to the Unarmed Protection of Civilians'" (New York, NY, March 23, 2012), http://www.un.org/en/ga/president/66/statements/peacekeeping230312.shtml.

38. Nassir Abdulaziz Al-Nasser, "Remarks at the Interactive Dialogue on the Responsibility to Protect" (New York, NY, September 5, 2012), http://www.un.org/en/ga/president/66/statements/.

39. Nassir Abdulaziz Al-Nasser, "Plenary Meeting of the General Assembly Agenda Item 64: 'Report of the Human Rights Council' on Syria" (New York, NY, February 13, 2012), http://www.un.org/en/ga/president/66/statements/syria130212.shtml.

40. Nassir Abdulaziz Al-Nasser, "Remarks at the 19th Session of the Human Rights Council" (Geneva, Switzerland, February, 27, 2012), http://www.un.org/en/ga/president/66/statements/geneva270212.shtml.

41. Nassir Abdulaziz Al-Nasser, "Before the Human Rights Council on the Urgent

Debate on Syria" (Geneva, Switzerland, February 28, 2012), http://www.un.org/en/ga/president/66/statements/syriahrc280212.shtml.

42. Nassir Abdulaziz Al-Nasser, "Remarks at the Briefing by the Joint Special Envoy on Syria" (New York, NY, April 5, 2012), http://www.un.org/en/ga/president/66/statements/syria050412.shtml.

43. United Nations Security Council, "Resolution 2042 (2012). Adopted by the Security Council at Its 6751st Meeting," April 14, 2012, http://www.un.org/ga/search/view_doc.asp?symbol=S/RES/2042(2012); United Nations Security Council, "Resolution 2043 (2012). Adopted by the Security Council at Its 6756th Meeting," April 21, 2012, http://www.un.org/ga/search/view_doc.asp?symbol=S/RES/2043(2012).

44. Nassir Abdulaziz Al-Nasser, "Remarks at the Plenary Meeting of the General Assembly on Events in the Syrian Arab Republic" (New York, NY, June 7, 2012), http://www.un.org/en/ga/president/66/statements/syria070612.shtml.

45. Nassir Abdulaziz Al-Nasser, "Meeting of the General Assembly of the United Nations on the Events in the Syrian Arab Republic" (New York, NY, August 3, 2012), http://www.un.org/en/ga/president/66/statements/syriaplenary030812.shtml.

46. Nassir Abdulaziz Al-Nasser, "Remarks at the Plenary Meeting of the General Assembly on the Situation in the Syrian Arab Republic" (New York, NY, September 4, 2012), http://www.un.org/en/ga/president/66/statements/.

47. United Nations General Assembly Resolution 60/288, "The United Nations Global Counter-Terrorism Strategy," September 20, 2006, http://daccess-dds-ny.un.org/doc/UNDOC/GEN/N05/504/88/PDF/N0550488.pdf?OpenElement.

48. Nassir Abdulaziz Al-Nasser, "Secretary-General's Symposium on International Counter-Terrorism Cooperation" (New York, NY, September 19, 2011), http://www.un.org/en/ga/president/66/statements/counterterrorism190911.shtml.

49. Nassir Abdulaziz Al-Nasser, "Remarks at the Seminar on Dialogue: Understanding and Countering the Appeal of Terrorism" (New York, NY, June 27, 2012), http://www.un.org/en/ga/president/66/statements/counterterrorism270612.shtml.

50. Nassir Abdulaziz Al-Nasser, "Closing Remarks at the Seminar on Dialogue: Understanding and Countering the Appeal of Terrorism" (New York, NY, June 27, 2012), http://www.un.org/en/ga/president/66/statements/counterterrorismclose270612.shtml.

51. International Atomic Energy Agency, "IAEA Action Plan on Nuclear Safety," June 2011, http://www.iaea.org/newscenter/focus/actionplan/reports/actionplanns130911.pdf.

52. Nassir Abdulaziz Al-Nasser, "On the Occasion of the High-Level Meeting on Nuclear Safety and Security" (New York, NY, September 22, 2011), http://www.un.org/en/ga/president/66/statements/nuclearsafety220901.shtml.

53. Nassir Abdulaziz Al-Nasser, "Remarks to the First Committee" (New York, NY, October 21, 2011), http://www.un.org/en/ga/president/66/statements/firstcom211011.shtml.

54. Nassir Abdulaziz Al-Nasser, "Remarks at the United Nations Disarmament Commission" (New York, NY, April 2, 2012), http://www.un.org/en/ga/president/66/statements/disarmament020412.shtml.

55. United Nations Office at Geneva, "Disarmament: An Introduction to the Conference," http://www.unog.ch/80256EE600585943/(httpPages)/BF18ABFEFE5D344 DC1256F3100311CE9?OpenDocument.

56. United Nations General Assembly Resolution 65/93, "Follow-Up to the High-Level Meeting Held on 24 September 2010: Revitalizing the Work of the Conference on Disarmament and Taking Forward Multilateral Disarmament Negotiations," January 11, 2011, http://www.un.org/ga/search/view_doc.asp?symbol=A/RES/65/93; United Nations General Assembly Resolution 66/66, "Revitalizing the Work of the Conference on Disarmament and Taking Forward Multilateral Disarmament Negotiations," January 12, 2012, http://www.un.org/ga/search/view_doc.asp?symbol=%20A/RES/66/66.

57. Nassir Abdulaziz Al-Nasser, "Remarks on the Occasion of the Opening of the Second Part of the 2012 Session of the Conference on Disarmament" (Geneva, Switzerland, May 15, 2012), http://www.un.org/en/ga/president/66/statements/disarmament150512.shtml.

58. CTBTO Preparatory Commission, "The Comprehensive Nuclear-Test-Ban Treaty," http://www.ctbto.org/fileadmin/content/treaty/treaty_text.pdf.

59. United Nations General Assembly Resolution 64/35, "International Day against Nuclear Tests," January 12, 2010, http://www.un.org/ga/search/view_doc.asp?symbol=A/RES/64/35.

60. Nassir Abdulaziz Al-Nasser, "Opening Remarks on the Informal Meeting of the General Assembly to Mark the Observance of the International Day against Nuclear Tests" (New York, NY, September 6, 2012), http://www.un.org/en/ga/president/66/statements/.

61. Republic of South Africa, Government Communication and Information System, "The Non-Aligned Movement: Background Information," http://www.nam.gov.za/background/background.htm#1.

62. Nassir Abdulaziz Al-Nasser, "Remarks at the Sixteenth Summit of the Non-Aligned Movement" (Tehran, Iran, August 30, 2012), http://www.un.org/en/ga/president/66/statements/nam300812.shtml.

63. United Nations Conference on the Illicit Trade in Small Arms and Light Weapons in All Its Aspects, "Programme of Action to Prevent, Combat and Eradicate the Illicit Trade in Small Arms and Light Weapons in All Its Aspects," July 20, 2001, http://cns.miis.edu/inventory/pdfs/aptsarms.pdf.

64. United Nations, "Outcome Document: Programme of Action to Prevent, Combat and Eradicate the Illicit Trade in Small Arms and Light Weapons in All Its Aspects," http://www.poa-iss.org/revcon2/documents/revcon-doc/rev1/draft-outcome-CRP3-rev3.pdf.

65. Nassir Abdulaziz Al-Nasser, "Remarks at the Second United Nations Conference

to Review Progress Made in the Implementation of the Programme of Action to Prevent, Combat and Eradicate the Illicit Trade in Small Arms and Light Weapons in All Its Aspects" (New York, NY, August 27, 2012), http://www.un.org/en/ga/president/66/statements/smallarms270812.shtml.

NOTES TO THE CONCLUSION

1. United Nations General Assembly Resolution 53/243, "Declaration and Programme of Action on the Culture of Peace," October 6, 1999, http://www.un.org/ga/search/view_doc.asp?symbol=A/RES/53/243.

2. Nassir Abdulaziz Al-Nasser, "Remarks at the Peace Bell Ceremony (New York, NY, September 15, 2011), http://www.un.org/en/ga/president/66/statements/peacebell-15092011.shtml.

3. Martin Luther King Jr., "Nobel Lecture: The Quest for Peace and Justice," December 11, 1964, http://www.nobelprize.org/nobel_prizes/peace/laureates/1964/king-lecture.html.

4. Nassir Abdulaziz Al-Nasser, "Opening Statement at the General Assembly High Level Forum on the Culture of Peace" (New York, NY, September 14, 2012), http://www.un.org/en/ga/president/66/statements/.

5. Nassir Abdulaziz Al-Nasser, "Remarks at Fordham University: Occasion on the Conferring of the Degree of Doctor of Laws, Honoris Causa on the PGA" (New York, NY, September 12, 2012), http://www.un.org/en/ga/president/66/statements/.

6. United Nations General Assembly Resolution 66/291, "Strengthening the Role of Mediation in the Peaceful Settlement of Disputes, Conflict Prevention and Resolution," October 15, 2012, http://www.un.org/ga/search/view_doc.asp?symbol=%20A/RES/66/291.

7. United Nations General Assembly Resolution 67/226, "Quadrennial Comprehensive Policy Review of the Operational Activities for Development of the United Nations System," January 22, 2013, http://www.un.org/ga/search/view_doc.asp?symbol=A/RES/67/226.

8. United Nations General Assembly Resolution 66/292, "Global Day of Parents," September 17, 2012, http://www.un.org/en/ga/search/view_doc.asp?symbol=%20A/RES/66/292; United Nations General Assembly Resolution 66/281, "International Day of Happiness," June 28, 2012, http://www.un.org/en/ga/search/view_doc.asp?symbol=%20A/RES/66/281.

INDEX

Abbas, Mahmoud, 15–16, 157
Accountability, 88
Accountability, Coherence and Transparency Group (ACT), Security Council reform model, 51
Accountable governance, 21–22
ACT. *See* Accountability, Coherence and Transparency Group
"Addressing Desertification, Land Degradation and Drought in the Context of Sustainable Development and Poverty Eradication," 79
"Addressing Excessive Price Volatility in Food and Related Commodity Markets," 76–77
Advisory Board of the Special Human Settlements Programme for the Palestinian People, 38
Africa development, 108–9
African Industrialization Day, 109
African Peer Review Mechanism, 109
African Union, 103; Security Council reform model, 51
African Union Mission in Somalia (AMISOM), 66; progress of, 68
Agenda 21, 72
Agricultural research, 104–5
Ahmed, Sheikh Sharif Sheikh, 66
Aid for Trade, 99
AIDS, 121–22
Ali, Adiweli Mohamed, 66
Alliance of Civilizations, xiv–xv, 158–59; dispute settlement role of, 40–43; effectiveness of, 9; establishment of, xv, 40–41; Fourth Forum, 30, 39, 41–42; Group of Friends, 41; innovative projects of, 41; Partners Forum of, 40; Qatar supporting, 9
Alliance of Small Island States, 107

Amendment on Voice and Participation, 11
AMISOM. *See* African Union Mission in Somalia
Annan, Kofi, 5, 141, 142, 143; on humanitarian intervention, 4
Arab Aid Consortium, 64
Arab Awakening, 3, 17–25; assisting, 21; dysfunctions, 20; energy access and, 82; exclusion and, 19; history of, 19–20; reform and, 20
Arab Spring, 3. *See also* Arab Awakening
Arms Trade Treaty, 15
ASEAN, 103
Autism, 123–24

Ban Ki-moon, ix–x, 14, 41, 167
Biodiversity loss, 83–86
Bouazizi, Mohamed, 18, 26
Bowler, Brian, 106
Brahimi, Lakhdar, 143
Brazil, Russia, India, China, and South Africa (BRICS), 11
BRICS. *See* Brazil, Russia, India, China, and South Africa
"Broadening the Concept of Peacekeeping: The Contribution of Civil Society to the Unarmed Protection of Civilians," 138
Buddhism, 6
Burk, Susan, 150

Cabral, José Filipe Moraes, 56
CD. *See* Conference on Disarmament
Centre of Excellence in Doha, 70
Christianity, 6
CIFA. *See* Convention of Independent Financial Advisors
Civil society, 16; coordinator for, 59
Climate change, 2, 83–86; adaptation strategies for, 85; in developing countries, 84;

ABOUT THE AUTHOR

Nassir Abdulaziz Al-Nasser served as the president of the 66th session of the United Nations General Assembly (2011–2012) and is currently the United Nations high representative for the Alliance of Civilizations. A veteran diplomat, he has contributed to advancing the multilateral agenda in the realms of peace and security, sustainable development, and South-South cooperation over a career spanning nearly four decades.